In a world distressed by pain and s-l^
Using a wealth of research, biblica
experiences, Debbie and Cathy enc
Far from being a kind word, or act,
lifestyle – to change the world one s\
cal starter tips to help us on our way. .. and
be inspired.

Cather ..., author of Journey With Me and God Isn't Finished With You Yet

A celebration of kindness: challenging, inspiring, and if we grasp its message – transformational.

Rob Parsons, OBE, speaker, author and founder and chairman of Care for the Family

To be honest, I have never read a whole book dedicated to the topic of kindness before. But reading *The Gift of Kindness* by Debbie Duncan and Cathy Le Feuvre has been a thoroughly enjoyable experience. This book beautifully combines healthy biblical and scientific analysis, sound practical advice and many examples of inspirational stories of kindness.

Reading this book has raised my understanding of what kindness really is to a whole new level and increased my motivation to live a life of intentional and habitual kindness. I believe that the topic of this book is a vitally important and timely message into where we are in our world right now.

You have been warned – reading this book could seriously improve your health.

John McEvoy, director of Elim Ministries (Republic of Ireland)

Kindness is one of those words we frequently overlook or skim past when reading the Bible as we search for guidance, blessing and instruction. The truth is, the ramifications of embracing this word in our daily lives are immense. Combining inspirational stories with insights drawn from psychological and neurological studies on the subject, Debbie and Cathy invite us to take practical steps both big and small to make kindness real and tangible in our world. It's a fascinating book. In these uncertain times the message of *The Gift of Kindness* is needed more than ever.

Dave Bilbrough, songwriter and worship leader

The Gift of Kindness is in your hands! This truly inspirational yet challenging exploration of a 'Tardis of a word', kindness, warms the heart, opens the eyes and beautifully and skilfully spurs the reader on to greater intentionality and influential kindly engagement with the world. Everyone should read this!

Commissioner Anthony Cotterill, Territorial Leader for The Salvation Army in the UK and the Republic of Ireland

This is a great read. Kindness as a 'fearsome not a fluffy thing' is described and explained so helpfully by Debbie, and Cathy brings a thorough exploration of one of the ways to wellbeing that I am so passionate about. With personal stories, practical suggestions and theological reflection this lovely book helps us all realise that kindness can change those who give it as well as those who receive it. Read this. It's beautiful. Let the kindness culture grow.

Ruth Rice, author of A–Z of Wellbeing *and director of Renew Wellbeing*

Kindness, as is said in this book, is a Tardis of a word. We think we know what it means, but it is in reality multi-faceted and as complex as we are as people. Yet it is so powerful both to receive and to give; a vehicle of genuine transformation as some of the stories in this helpful and accessible book demonstrate. Appealing as it does to both our heads and our hearts, by helping us learn more about what it really means and also encouraging us in practical ways to become kinder, I warmly commend it to you.

Jeannie Kendall, speaker and writer, author of
Finding Our Voice *and* Held in Your Bottle

What if kindness is the antidote to much of the stress and struggle we face? What if simple actions and words could unlock the best in people and projects? After reading this book, I'm fully convinced of the extraordinary potential and power of kindness. I can't recommend it highly enough.

Cathy Madavan, writer, speaker, broadcaster and author of
Digging for Diamonds *and* Irrepressible

This book plunges deeply into the meaning of kindness, from the origins of the word to anecdotes to the positive effects of the action.

I cannot imagine anyone who, after reading this book, will not seek to be more kind towards individuals, nations and the world, in our shared humanity.

It's not just a great read, it's a real challenge!

Fiona Castle, retired dancer, writer, campaigner
and wife of the late Roy Castle

When someone is unkind, you spot it immediately. Why do we so often overlook, or fail to properly value, someone who has developed the consistent practice of actually being kind beyond the norm? Debbie and Cathy have done us a great favour by shining a spotlight on one of the fruits of the Spirit that is truly transformative – for us and others!

Paul Harcourt, National Leader of New Wine England

The Gift of Kindness

The transforming power of being kind

Debbie Duncan and Cathy Le Feuvre

28 27 26 25 24 23 22 7 6 5 4 3 2 1

First published 2022 by Authentic Media Limited,
PO Box 6326, Bletchley, Milton Keynes, MK1 9GG.
authenticmedia.co.uk

British Library Cataloguing in Publication Data
A catalogue record for this book is available from the British Library.
ISBN: 978-1-78893-244-8
978-1-78893-245-5 (e-book)

Cover design by Mercedes Piñera
Printed and bound by CPI Group (UK) Ltd, Croydon, CR0 4YY

Foreword

Kindness is making the headlines again. In August 2021 the BBC, in conjunction with a team of researchers from the University of Sussex, launched a research study looking at the subject.[1] Many of its findings are echoed here, in these pages. It became known as 'The Kindness Test' and is the largest in-depth study on kindness in the world, with more than 60,000 people aged 18–99 taking part from 144 countries. The results were analysed and shared during March 2022 in a series on BBC Radio 4 called *The Anatomy of Kindness*, presented by the author and psychologist Claudia Hammond.[2]

The study and radio series suggest that kindness could be good for you, while highlighting perceived barriers to kindness. Participants felt that they did not have enough time to be kind (57.5%); some were worried that kindness could be misconstrued (65.9%); some felt that social media made being kind harder (52.3%); some felt they did not have the opportunity to show kindness (42.1%) and just over a quarter of participants felt kindness could be seen as weakness (27.6%).[3] What are we to make of all of this and the other fascinating findings of the research?[4]

Kindness matters. From the academics exploring it, to the Ukrainian refugees who, at the time of writing, are streaming out of their country looking for a kind face and a place to stay and millions of people across Europe opening their homes and hearts towards them, kindness is both a powerful need and a powerful gift. Parents need it, kids need it, grieving families need it, exhausted NHS workers need it. Human beings everywhere need it. In the words of Aesop, of fable fame, 'no act of kindness, no matter how small, is ever wasted'.[5] Kindness lifts the heart, cheers the soul, gives strength to the weak and comfort to the broken-hearted. Whose life is not enriched by it?

Debbie and Cathy remind us that kindness is like a Tardis – there is so much more in it than a single definition can set out. Their work reminds me that a world bereft of kindness is a world that is less beautiful, less hopeful, less appealing. A world that is bereft of kindness is just less.

I have experienced a lack of kindness – and it hurts. Growing up, I was bullied at school and thought I wouldn't survive it. Home was not always a kind place. Northern Ireland, famed for its hospitality and welcome, was not always a kind community, particularly if you were from 'the other' side of the community – whatever that means. When kindness is absent, harshness is present, legalism and judgementalism can run riot and belittling can reduce human beings to things. A lack of kindness stings your soul, leaving a gaping wound in your spirit. I am sorry to say that I have been unkind far too often and have regretted it every time, because when you experience or show unkindness you always regret it. So why do we do it? Perhaps our desire to get even is stronger than our desire to show mercy? Are we bad at controlling our reactions? We are fallen and broken people and we live in a fallen and broken world – maybe that is the reason? Whatever the reasons may be (the chapter in this book on whether or not kindness is innate is fascinating), a kinder world is a better world.

From its ancient roots in blessing and the Hebrew idea of *chesed* to the BBC / University of Sussex research, kindness continues to intrigue, beckon and baffle us. I want to live in a kinder world and one day I will. Swords will be beaten into ploughshares. Nations will not invade other nations. Hatred will not win. Darkness will not last forever. Pain will end. Shame will be dissolved in the light of the coming of Christ. As I journey towards the wonderful fulfilment of God's ultimate purposes, however, I want to grow in my own kindness. My problem is that I know, deep within my heart, that I cannot muster kindness up myself. I need a source for kindness that will always be there. That source is Jesus Christ, who has promised to grow the fruit of kindness in the hearts of all who will let him.

Maybe the world, families, churches, workplaces, communities and nations can be kinder? And maybe, just maybe, that is only possible when we let the seed of kindness take root in the soil of our own souls?

May this book help that seed be planted in each of our souls.

Revd Malcolm J. Duncan F.R.S.A.
County Down
March 2022.

Contents

Foreword by Malcolm Duncan v

1 What is Kindness? 1
2 The Biblical Perspective on Kindness 17
3 The Life of Jesus 29
4 The Science of Kindness 49
5 The Impact of Kindness on the Individual 61
6 The Impact of Kindness on Society 73
7 The Rise of Kindness During the Pandemic 88
8 Do We Have Innate Kindness? 105
9 Creating a Kindness Culture 119
10 Living Out Kindness: Looking to the Future 137

A Final Reflection on Kindness 153
Bibliography 155
Notes 164

1

What is Kindness?

Debbie Duncan

The essence of love is kindness; and indeed it may best be defined as passionate kindness: kindness, so to speak, run mad and become importunate and violent.

Robert Louis Stevenson[1]

Why is kindness popular?

The idea that kindness is a new idea, a recent trend adopted by our society, is wrong. Certainly, since the outbreak of COVID-19 and the resulting pandemic, kindness is experiencing a boom but even before that there have been campaigns to increase kindness for several years, including the ever-popular idea of 'acts of random kindness'.

We have come to understand that acts of kindness have the potential to make the world a happier place. If someone is kind to you it can boost your confidence and increase your happiness, optimism and hope. Acts of kindness can also lead to the good deed being repeated – changing our communities, even our world.

Definition

Let's go back to basics and first ask the simple question: 'What is kindness?' Well, it is a noun, and is 'the quality of being generous, helpful, and caring about other people, or an act showing this quality'.[2] The researchers Cole-King and Gilbert have defined kindness as being 'sensitivity to the distress of . . . others with a commitment to try and do something about it'.[3] There is a saying that describes 'Kindness [as a] language which the deaf can hear and the blind can see'.[4]

The origin of the word

Of course, kindness is not a new concept. In fact, the Greek philosopher Aristotle defines kindness as 'helpfulness towards someone in need, not in return for anything, nor for the advantage of the helper himself, but for that of the person helped'.[5]

There are several schools of thought about the origins of the word. One is that it appears to be related to the idea of 'kinship'. Kindness is therefore an indication that you are recognising someone as being like you so you treat them like you would be treated.

Other researchers suggest that the word kindness developed from the Old English word 'kyndnes' meaning 'nation' or 'produce, increase'. It is also thought to come from the Middle English word 'kindenes' which means 'noble deeds' or 'well-born' or 'well-bred'. The idea was that well-bred people possessed the quality of natural kindness. I can however think of many historic noblemen and women who were the very opposite of well-bred and kind!

In 2006 the journalist York Membery, working for the BBC, asked ten leading historians who they believed to have had the most malign influence on the country.[6] The list includes a king, a prime minister and even a couple of church ministers.

Professor John Hudson of the University of St Andrews nominated Thomas Becket (c. 1120–70), who was the Archbishop of Canterbury. He divided England and was a 'marmite' figure – someone who inspired both devotion and detestation. He is not someone that I would call a kind person.

'The lawe of kynde' has a different meaning. It is a concept mentioned in a poem called *Piers Plowman* written in the late fourteenth century by William Langland.[7] The poem describes a vision or a religious experience in which different objects represent good and evil. Langland highlights that people have an innate desire to love God and their neighbour. Langland's 'lawe of kynde' considers the structure of justice as reciprocity or a balanced exchange of outcome for action. Judgement can be turned on its head by bringing the claims of the one to be judged to bear upon the decision of the one who judges. God is depicted in the poem as 'Kynde'.

Historical perspectives

The definition of 'kind' has changed through the centuries in its meaning and purpose. One example is that in the Victorian era, kindness became feminised and synonymous with sentimentality. Men feared that too much kindness would cloud their thinking on important matters, and yet this was still a season of great altruism and activism. Examples of those who epitomise acts of kindness from this era include Florence Nightingale, Thomas Barnardo and Joseph Rowntree.

The German philosopher Nietzsche believed that kindness itself held medicinal properties. In fact, he called it 'the most curative herb and agent in human intercourse'.[8]

But kindness is more than just 'being nice' or even thinking of others before ourselves. Although that, of course, is important, scientifically and anthropologically kindness is believed to be the single most significant quality that distinguishes us as humans. It marks our shared humanity. Anthropologists believe it's the evolutionary key to humankind's survival and development over many thousands of years.

It's a way we show and develop our cultures and our lives as humans. Performing acts of kindness, with no thought of a return will, bit by bit, act by act, prove life-changing for giver and receiver alike. Kindness in this respect can change the world.

Kindness and popular culture

In 1998 the World Kindness Movement launched World Kindness Day. This annual celebration on 13 November encourages people to make the world a better place through good deeds. The World Kindness Movement is a coalition of nations' kindness NGOs and was celebrated across the world, and it's captured the imagination of people and governments.

In 2010 the New South Wales Federation of Parents and Citizens Association in Australia wrote to the Minister of The NSW Department of Education to place World Kindness Day on the NSW School Calendar.

In the UK Kindness Day was also set up in 2010 by the British novelist and humanitarian Louise Burfitt-Dons and David Jamilly, a social entrepreneur and humanitarian. David founded The Good Deeds Organisation in 2005 and set up the not-for-profit organisation Kindness UK in 2011. You can visit their website and find examples of acts of kindness across the world,[9] like the 10,000 free chocolate bars handed out at London train stations by Kindness UK. The Singapore Kindness Movement gave out 30,000 Gerberas and World Kindness Australia conducted an enormous Kindness Hug on Bondi Beach.

In 2007, in a response to the London bombings, one individual approached two primary schools near where they lived and invited them to participate in a programme she devised: 'The Act of Kindness'.

This programme, while it began as one individual's response in the UK, fitted in so well with the values-based education of Australia that it was adopted into the nine values identified by the Federal Government there. By 2010, more than forty schools were participating in the programme.

Brands and campaigns

In 2015 it became popular for brands to run random Acts of Kindness campaigns. One of them was 'But First, Let Me Take a Selflessie' run by Toyota. They launched a campaign that gives people the chance to do something kind for someone else. They did this using selfies! So, in December 2015, they launched on #GivingTuesday where every single selfie with a hashtag on Instagram with #Selflessie triggered a $50 donation from Toyota to the Boys & Girls Clubs of America. Initially they planned to donate up to $250,000 but this soon increased to $750,000.

Recently the fundraising platform 'Go Fund Me' used its platform to promote New Yorkers as kind as they donate so much money through the platform. Their campaign is 'The New York State of Kind', which seems to be a play on words from the Billy Joel song 'New York State of Mind'.

This use of rebranding and focusing on kindness seems to be trending in the UK too. The *Daily Mirror* news brand has made a 'commitment to report more hopeful news' and launched '1000 acts of kindness' in June 2021, calling the UK a nation of kindness.[10]

In 2021 Unilever started a TV ad campaign here in the UK for their soap products called 'Simple'.[11] They highlight that being kind is an intrinsic part of being human. Their promise about their products is based on the premise that kindness is at the heart of everything they do. On Sunday 4 July the UK hosted Thank You Day 2021 and Unilever supported it. It was a response to the work and support of people during the COVID-19 pandemic. Companies have certainly taken an interest in kindness and what it is as the public interest in it has increased. They may be trying to commercialise it, but we are glad that they are highlighting kindness.

Pay it forward

In 2000 an American film directed by Mimi Leder called *Pay It Forward* hit the box office and grossed $55 million worldwide. The main plot of the film is the idea that the characters should do three good deeds for others, ultimately creating a social movement that could make the world a better place.

The film is loosely based on the book by the same name written by Catherine Ryan Hyde (more about her later).[12] The film led to many pay it forward initiatives. The concept of pay it forward is actually an old one and the phrase became popular after Lily Hardy Hammond mentioned it in her book, *In the Garden of Delight*, published in 1916.[13]

In 2000 Catherine Ryan Hyde founded the Pay it Forward Foundation in the USA. Its main aim is to be a catalyst to inspire growth for the pay it forward philosophy and acts of kindness among strangers, generating a ripple effect of kindness acts from one person to the next, one community to the next, and around the world.[14] In 2007, International Pay It Forward Day was founded in Australia. It has now spread to seventy countries and is estimated to have inspired more than 5 million acts of kindness.

Despite the ever-growing movement to see more kindness in the world, not everyone has felt that they have seen or experienced more kindness, particularly during the COVID-19 pandemic. Some people found it a tough and challenging time coping with shielding, illness, or death and loss. What we can agree is that most of us want to be kinder people.

A kind identity

I believe that people like to think that they are kind. For some people they seem to have innate or natural kindness. We can all think of people that we consider as naturally kind people.

However, we can also develop a kind identity.

The characteristics that constitute people's identities fall into five broad categories. Four of these categories are features of identity that distinguish us from others on the basis of physical characteristics, personal attributes, relationships, or membership of groups. The fifth category are the identity characteristics that reflect a connection with other people or the world. We can therefore classify ourselves as having a kind identity if it is a distinguishing characteristic.

Jesus is kind in the way he interacts with people, by his word and deeds. He has a kind identity. His kind identity is rich, explosive, extraordinary. 'Kind' is not a plain word like 'nice' or 'beige'. It is bold, colourful, worth dying for. I want to be like that – I want to be known as being kind.

The author and lifestyle coach Marcia Sirota in the HuffPost suggests that there is a distinct difference between being nice and being kind.[15] She suggests that kindness comes from someone who is confident, compassionate and comfortable with themselves; that they are loving and give out of the goodness of their heart. In contrast to this she suggests that at the root of what she calls 'extreme niceness' are feelings of inadequacy and the need to get approval from others.

The famous nineteenth-century author Robert Louis Stevenson said, 'The essence of love is kindness; and indeed, it may best be defined as passionate kindness: kindness, so to speak, run mad and become importunate and violent.'[16]

Kindness is so much closer to love than just being nice.

What are kind people like?

There are so many similar definitions of kindness. Analysing them, I have concluded that there are common characteristics which define kind people. These are some things that I have found out about kind people. You may disagree with them. Ultimately the kindest person I know is Jesus.

- Kind people are giving and have no ulterior motives. They don't care if people like them.
- Kind people show genuine love and care.
- Kind people are interested in you as a person.
- Kind people have positive self-esteem. They love others as they love themselves.
- Kind people are often happy people.

When I think about kind people, I have an image of someone who is compassionate of others. They are considerate of other people's feelings and are not self-centred. If that's what it means to be kind, I want to have a kind identity. I want to know how this fruit of the Spirit can be grown in my life. I know that I can become kinder.

A change of perspective

On the 28 December 2020 I received my PCR test result informing me I had COVID-19. The first few weeks of January were really tough. All my immediate family ended up with the virus. My husband, Malcolm, also had Covid and was waiting for a pacemaker. Then we received the news that my dad had COVID-19 too. He is in a care home where thirteen out of thirty-two residents eventually passed away due to the disease. I found I was fighting Covid, coping with the unknown and dealing with fear and anxiety about it all. These were well-founded fears that were built around me like a brick wall.

Thankfully Psalm 18:28–29 says:

> You, LORD, keep my lamp burning; my God turns my darkness into light. With your help I can advance against a troop; with my God I can scale a wall.

In late March 2021 I realised that I was feeling quite low. I asked God to help me scale the wall around me. God started removing the bricks one by one.

One night I could not sleep and prayed about it. I realised that instead of looking in on my world and feeling like I was hemmed in, I had to start facing outward, looking at the community around me. I started asking, 'What did *they* need?' I felt God was challenging me about my perspective.

About this time, I had a hospital appointment and called into a supermarket on the way home. There was an old lady in front of me who was buying food for her supper. I got the impression she was lonely and probably came to the shop every day. There were buckets of daffodils for sale at the sales desk; she looked at them and moved on. I bought my shopping, bought a couple of bunches of flowers and tried to find her. I handed her the flowers and heard her tell all the people around her that someone had bought her some. Her face was beaming, and I felt less hemmed in. Another brick had been removed.

So, through Lent 2021 I made the decision to carry out acts of kindness to those around me as I reflected on what Easter meant to me. Each time I prayed and did something, another brick fell down and the light shone into my world. I also found that as I was intentional about being kind, I felt happier, and it became easier to do.

Joseph Robert (Bob) Kerrey is an American politician who served as the thirty-fifth governor of Nebraska and a United States senator. Prior to entering politics, he served in the Vietnam War as a United States Navy SEAL officer. He was injured in battle and was awarded the Medal of Honour for heroism in combat. He is attributed as saying, 'Unexpected kindness is the most powerful, least costly, and most underrated agent of human change.'[17]

My acts of kindness not only changed those I was kind to, but they also changed my own life.

Cathy Le Feuvre

The importance of kindness in the world

Throughout my life I've witnessed and experienced kindness on many occasions, and in many people. Living as a child of Christian leaders in The Salvation Army, who then moved to Africa when I was quite young, I was aware of the kindnesses of others. I learned the importance of kindness and the implications of my behaviour and actions.

Our family had little in the way of money and resources most of the time, but often we benefited from the generosity of others, and I also saw the way my parents shared what little they had with others. Before we left for Africa and my parents were church leaders, I remember going down to breakfast and finding a 'gentleman of the road' at our table, my dad having met him the previous evening and brought him in from the rain and cold, with an invitation to sleep on a mattress in the garage to prevent him freezing on the streets. In Africa, a Boxing Day picnic and barbecue was held on our remote farm where many local Salvation Army and other friends gathered with our family, everyone bringing something to the table to share.

If you've ever got involved with one of those 'sharing' lunches or suppers, you've seen kindness in action because there will always be those who are unable to bring food to the table, but are welcome to sit down to eat anyway.

Throughout my life I've witnessed people spending hours delivering food parcels and reaching out to others who they don't even know. In fact, on the day my dad passed away, or as we say in The Salvation Army, was 'Promoted to Glory', he had spent the afternoon picking up food from the Marks & Spencer's supermarket which was still in date but could not be sold in the store, so it could be packed up and delivered to those in need.

As a journalist and broadcaster, I've been privileged to witness so many kindnesses down the years and especially in my time as a 'faith' producer and presenter, working in programming which reflects faith and Christian communities, I have been humbled by what I have seen and reported on. The churches and individuals running foodbanks, looking after homeless people, caring for victims of trafficking and domestic violence, and families in crisis. Not to mention those just making themselves available to offer a listening ear or a shoulder to cry on.

Of course, we know that good deeds are not confined to people of faith, but as Christians these sorts of kind actions are what Christ calls us to do, and while some may see it as their 'duty' or even their job to do this work, I would say that when we have Jesus in our lives this is something that could begin to come naturally. It's an example of that kindness imperative that Jesus empowers us to live out. When we ask ourselves 'what would Jesus do?' then the answer has to be – be kind, compassionate and loving, not to draw attention to ourselves but just because it's what we are called to be and because it feels natural to do it, even if it means a sacrifice for ourselves.

And what we do doesn't have to be ground-breaking. Acts of kindness and compassion come in all shapes and sizes.

Making a difference

During the coronavirus pandemic it was part of my job, then working for BBC Radio Jersey, the local BBC radio station in the Channel Islands, to help share 'Make a Difference' stories. This campaign was quite simple, really; it just gathered stories of people who were reaching out to others, mostly for little or no reward or recognition. We shared those stories on the radio to inspire others and, sometimes when appropriate, to gather support for those causes.

No sooner had the first lockdown begun in March 2020 than we saw the setting up of a special Facebook page – 'Coronavirus Jersey – Acts of Kindness' – a grassroots campaign to connect islanders and share resources and messages of support. It also helped people to share their needs without feeling ashamed, and this resulted in the most tremendous outpouring of kindness. All over our lovely little island of Jersey, rainbows appeared in windows, a sign of hope. Children painted little pebbles which you would come across in random spots around the island as a reminder of love and kindness and friendship. People stepped up to deliver goods to those shut in at home, to volunteer, to share what they had with those who had less.

At the invitation of the Government of Jersey, The Salvation Army church and charity movement locally established and ran the island's foodbank and what resulted was an outpouring of support and love – they were inundated with not just messages of support but donations of food and cash and manpower. The hairdresser who couldn't open his shop instead spent his time working in the foodbank. There were many volunteers, most with no connection to the church, who stepped up to fill food bags and drive around delivering them safely to those who could not leave home. It was a real community effort!

One story from the pandemic that sticks in my mind is the ice cream van man who, in May 2020, parked his vehicle in front of the hospital and gave free ice creams to all those health professionals and others working in that building to keep us healthy and safe. And he did this on his own birthday! What a joy-bringer! We will read more about this later in the book.

It is easy to be cynical about the world, to seek out the negative in people and situations. But we don't have to look far to see the good that others do every day and, especially for those of us who aspire or claim to be Christians, if only a little of that inspires *us* to go do the same, then we will be truly living the Jesus way.

> Therefore, as God's chosen people, holy and dearly loved, clothe yourselves with compassion, kindness, humility, gentleness and patience.
>
> *Colossians 3:12*

There's that word right at the heart of it all – *kindness*!

Understanding what kindness means to us

As we work through this book, we'll hear many inspirational stories which I hope will encourage us to be truly kind in our behaviours, outlook, attitudes and spirit.

If we're thinking about creating a kinder world it can be good to start somewhere simple in all our relationships and thinking. To find kindness in unexpected places where we might not ordinarily go, and to discover kindness in the day-to-day of our lives.

We're on warning here – that may mean a close interrogation of our own motivations and mindset, and that may be challenging for some of us.

We will learn how important kindness has been and can be in our world and we'll begin to understand a bit more about how kindness can affect not just our personal relationships, face-to-face and online. I also hope this will throw a spotlight on how kindness might be part of other areas of life including business and commerce, politics, even media.

While we might not yet have many structures in place which promote kindness in these areas and it might appear there are insurmountable problems facing us, we can take heart from the kindnesses we saw during the height of the pandemic in 2020 and 2021. Those kindnesses came most commonly from the hearts of individuals rather than from corporate bodies. They were a human response to the needs of others, and they inspired us all.

This unprecedented time in human history has also created, or revived, an interest in kindness, and my hope is that as we realise or learn again the importance of kindness at all levels, as we observe and learn from the truly kind people in our midst, and as we see how we can be part of the movement to create a better, kinder culture, we will also begin to see the kind of world which God wishes for his creation.

Practical pointers

So, as we step into this kindness journey, where to start?

We would suggest that you keep a journal through this journey of discovery. Journaling is not just about writing down your memories, but it is a strategy that helps us reflect and learn. There are many people who have used journaling to enrich their lives, such as Queen Victoria, Ralph Waldo Emerson, John Steinbeck and Ben Franklin.

Record your journey and you can go back and be reminded of what happened along the way.

Our prayer is that not only do you learn about how enriching the gift of kindness is to other people, but also for your own life.

Summary

We have looked at the definition of kindness and we have only scratched the surface of what it means. I (Debbie) recently had a conversation with my husband about what kindness means. I was trying to explain that I feel the English translation of the word does not encompass what it means. It was like trying to describe a beautiful scene with five words. He looked at me and smiling he said, 'Kindness is a Tardis of a word.' For those of you who are not Doctor Who fans – the Doctor's time machine is infinitely larger on the inside than on the outside.

Prayer

Thank you, Lord, that you demonstrate what kindness really is.
We are amazed at what you have done for us.
Help us to allow the fruit of kindness to grow in our lives.
We want to be known as being kind people.
Show us how we can be intentional about kindness.
In Jesus' name.
Amen.

2

The Biblical Perspective on Kindness

Debbie Duncan

> *Be kind and compassionate to one another, forgiving each other, just as in Christ God forgave you.*
>
> Ephesians 4:32

I must admit I was a little nervous about writing this chapter. It was the topic I thought about and reflected on for the longest period. I think it was because I don't want to miss anything. If I do, then please forgive me. I am not saying I am an expert on this topic – I am writing it as a disciple who is still learning more each day about life. I hope it encompasses all I have learned, and I am sure there is so much more that can be added.

In the New Testament the word 'kindness' is written in Greek: *chrēstotēs*. It means tender concern and uprightness. It refers to a kindness of heart and the kindness of action.

Most of what I knew about kindness from the Bible was from the well-known passage in Paul's book to the Galatians where he talks about living in step with God's Spirit. The fifth fruit of the Spirit is listed as kindness. It certainly is not easy to always be kind, especially to those who have hurt us.

Galatians 5:13–26 says:

> You, my brothers and sisters, were called to be free. But do not use your freedom to indulge the flesh; rather, serve one another humbly in love. For the entire law is fulfilled in keeping this one command: 'Love your neighbour as yourself.' If you bite and devour each other, watch out or you will be destroyed by each other.
>
> So I say, live by the Spirit, and you will not gratify the desires of the flesh. For the flesh desires what is contrary to the Spirit, and the Spirit what is contrary to the flesh. They are in conflict with each other, so that you are not to do whatever you want. But if you are led by the Spirit, you are not under the law.
>
> The acts of the flesh are obvious: sexual immorality, impurity and debauchery; idolatry and witchcraft; hatred, discord, jealousy, fits of rage, selfish ambition, dissensions, factions and envy; drunkenness, orgies, and the like. I warn you, as I did before, that those who live like this will not inherit the kingdom of God.
>
> But the fruit of the Spirit is love, joy, peace, forbearance, *kindness*, goodness, faithfulness, gentleness and self-control. Against such things there is no law. Those who belong to Christ Jesus have crucified the flesh with its passions and desires. Since we live by the Spirit, let us keep in step with the Spirit. Let us not become conceited, provoking and envying each other. (emphasis mine)

If there is a verse in the Bible that sums up kindness, then for me it is this verse – Ephesians 4:32 – which we read at the start of this chapter. I think we can only really experience the full beauty of kindness when we have come to know that kindness that God extends to us through his Son Jesus.

In Titus 3:3–5 it also says, 'At one time we too were foolish, disobedient, deceived and enslaved by all kinds of passions and pleasures. We lived in malice and envy, being hated and hating one another. But when the kindness and love of God our Saviour appeared, he saved us, not because of righteous things we had done, but because of his mercy.'

This kindness is explosive. It's not meek and humble – it blasts a huge hole in the bleakness of death, letting in light, tearing down curtains, rolling away huge boulders. It takes command of death and casts it aside. It's powerful, extraordinary, mind-blowing. It changes the lives of men and women, boys and girls who have come to know that God is kind, sending his son to die the worst death imaginable for us.

One of my favourite Old Testament books is that of Ruth. I think it sums up a lot of what scriptures tell us about kindness.

The story of Ruth

The name 'Ruth' means compassion, and this is central to the book. It is also an important book in the Hebrew Bible and is included in the third division or the 'Writings'. According to Jewish traditions, the book is written by Samuel, but we don't know a lot about the author. We do know it is a beautiful story which introduces us to Ruth, the great-grandmother of King David and a relative of Jesus.

It is thought to be set during the period of the Judges of Israel between 1160–110 BC. We are told at the start of the book that there was a man called Elimelek from Bethlehem in Judah who moved to Moab with his wife Naomi and their two sons because of great famine that had affected the land. Even though the central figure is Ruth, the book is written from Naomi, her mother-in-law's point of view. Naomi's husband dies after their move to Moab, and she is left with two sons who marry Moabite girls, Orpah and Ruth. She grieves her husband and then she loses her two sons. Naomi decides that all there is in Moab is death and loss, so she makes the decision to head back to her homeland.

> Then Naomi said to her two daughters-in-law, 'Go back, each of you, to your mother's home. May the Lord show you kindness, as you have shown kindness to your dead husbands and to me. May the Lord grant that each of you will find rest in the home of another husband.'
>
> Then she kissed them goodbye and they wept aloud and said to her, 'We will go back with you to your people.' But Naomi said, 'Return home, my daughters.'
>
> *Ruth 1:8–11*

Orpah says her goodbyes and exits stage left. We are expecting Ruth to do the same thing, but she doesn't. Naomi expects it too. In fact, Ruth does the opposite and declares her undying devotion to her mother-in-law.

> But Ruth replied, 'Don't urge me to leave you or to turn back from you. Where you go I will go, and where you stay I will stay. Your people will be my people and your God my God. Where you die I will die, and there I will be buried. May the Lord deal with me, be it ever so severely, if even death separates you and me.' When Naomi realised that Ruth was determined to go with her, she stopped urging her.
>
> So the two women went on until they came to Bethlehem . . .
>
> *Ruth 1:16–19*

They set off on a journey to Bethlehem and arrive just as the harvest of barley was starting. A reminder of another journey to Bethlehem. This time it was two women travelling the fifty-odd miles. They had no male relative to protect them, which would have been unusual. I wonder if they attached themselves to a caravan crossing the terrain? Two widows – one heading to an unknown land, one travelling the journey she had made before as a younger woman full of hope and expectation with her husband by her side. No wonder she told her friends in Bethlehem to call her 'bitter' (v. 20).

Naomi and Ruth had no great announcement upon their arrival. No angels or shepherds, although they probably wondered if there was room for them at the inn. They had no one financially supporting them so Ruth suggests that she glean in the fields behind the barley harvesters. In Leviticus 19:9–10 and Deuteronomy 24:19–22 God had commanded that the landowners leave anything harvesters didn't pick up so the poor, the widowed, the foreigners, and the fatherless had a supply of food. One day Ruth is working hard when the owner of the field and a relative of Naomi's dead husband sees her.

Boaz is kind to Ruth, giving her freedom to drink from his water jars as she worked. Ruth was stunned that she was treated in such a kind manner and asked why the man was so kind to her. Boaz informs her that he had heard of Ruth's devotion to Naomi. He even feeds her from his own table and makes sure his workers leave choice grain for her to pick up. He sees in Ruth someone who is kind and compassionate. In Ruth 2:11–12 it says:

> Boaz replied, 'I've been told all about what you have done for your mother-in-law since the death of your husband – how you left your father and mother and your homeland and came to live with a people you did not know before. May the LORD repay you for what you have done. May you be richly rewarded by the LORD, the God of Israel, under whose wings you have come to take refuge.'

The book and the story of Ruth teaches us about genuine love and sacrifice. There are so many reminders of the greatest gift we have been given through the birth of a baby in Bethlehem many years later. It also reminds us that God wants a kinder, fairer society.

Think of the law that allowed Ruth to glean the field. We can read about it more in Leviticus 19:9–10 and Deuteronomy 24:19–22, as mentioned above. God had to remind his people twice that we are to care for the stranger and those in need. The importance of protecting and being kind to the most vulnerable in society was enshrined in their law. If we try to live out God's laws and reflect his character, our society is richer for it.

God wants us to be missional, to be a community known for its kindness to others.

God's kindness is stronger than death!

Naomi experienced terrible loss. Imagine losing your husband and two sons. She also thought she was going to lose her daughters-in-law. They wouldn't want to follow where she was going . . . would they? Naomi smelled of death and loss. Naomi tells Ruth to stop calling her Naomi but to refer to her as 'Mara' which means 'bitter place in the desert' (Ruth 1:20). She may have felt like she was in the desert, but she did not lose her faith.

Death did not stop Ruth from also making a choice to follow the God of Israel. Kindness is stronger than death and we are reminded of this in the New Testament – in Romans 8:38–39:

> For I am convinced that neither death nor life, neither angels nor demons, neither the present nor the future, nor any powers, neither height nor depth, nor anything else in all creation, will be able to separate us from the love of God that is in Christ Jesus our Lord.

God's kindness leads to life if we accept his gift to us.

God's kindness leads us to follow him

Ruth chose to follow Naomi's God. Ruth begged Naomi to allow her to emigrate to Judah and follow her. She turns her back on the gods of Moab and chooses to follow the God of Israel. In fact, she declares a solemn vow or covenant before Yahweh that she will stay with Naomi. She knows God's name. Perhaps she had to come to know and respect God through her Jewish family. We don't know. What we do know is that witnessing God's great kindness to us should lead us to repent and follow him. We are reminded of God's great covenant promises towards us.

Ruth chose to enter a covenant, both with Naomi and with the Lord. These covenants gave her access to blessings from the Lord and a right to a redeemer. Having made a covenant, Boaz was obligated to redeem her. The result of this redemption eventually led to the birth of King David, and ultimately to the birth of Jesus. This was all part of God's redemptive plan.

In the book of Romans 2:4 the apostle Paul says, 'Or do you show contempt for the riches of his kindness, forbearance and patience, not realising that God's kindness is intended to lead you to repentance?'

For years people have been searching for the answer to all life's questions. In Douglas Adams' tongue-in-cheek book, *The Hitchhiker's Guide to the Galaxy*, the hapless Arthur Dent discovers the supercomputer Deep Thought. He is told that the answer to the ultimate question of life is the number 42.

But from a Christian perspective, the answer to life's questions is simply, and profoundly, this: because God loves us and is kind and compassionate, he gave his Son to die in our place. We can respond to his great kindness and accept this gift. The other side of the equation is that because he is kind to us, we can be kind to other people. We can love people.

We can forgive people more than forty-two times, more than seventy-seven times (Matt. 18:22). His Spirit helps us do this.

Kindness looks like something

Boaz shows us that kindness is not just reactive but that kindness looks like something. He too stepped up and repaid Ruth for her kindness, but he also became her kinsman redeemer and her husband; astonishing, as Ruth wasn't the kind of woman his own mother would be happy with. After all, she was a Moabitess, a member of Israel's enemy tribe. Despite this, Boaz married the young widow Ruth, a woman from the wrong side of the tracks. He had seen a great kindness in her. Often kindness begets kindness.

In Ruth 2:20 Naomi speaks to Ruth about Boaz: '"The Lord bless him!" Naomi said to her daughter-in-law. "He has not stopped showing his kindness to the living and the dead." She added, "That man is our close relative; he is one of our guardian-redeemers."'

Boaz chose to show kindness to Ruth because of how she treated his relation.

Kindness can be challenging

Kindness can, however, be challenging – there can be a cost involved. For Ruth it was choosing to leave her homeland and travel more than fifty miles. Moab is in the modern-day state of Jordan where the land is mountainous and lies along the eastern side of the Dead Sea. Any journey would be in a boat across difficult waters or over land across rugged terrain. We don't think twice about making a fifty-mile journey these days. But then, it meant making a seven-to-ten-day journey by foot. They would not have the money for any other mode of transport.

Ruth was moving to another country, leaving behind her friends and family. She was leaving the place where her husband, her father-in-law and brother-in-law were buried. She would not be able to go home every weekend and have Sunday dinner with her parents, if they were still alive.

Sometimes it is hard to be kind.

Sometimes, the kindest action or word can also feel like they are anything but kind. We can have a fear of hurting someone's feelings or being perceived as 'difficult' when we speak the truth. There is an expectation in society that we should be nice, but being 'nice' doesn't mean you are honest and true. Being kind is not the same as being nice. Being 'nice' is considered as being agreeable but 'kind' stems from benevolence. Benevolence is kindness – the generosity of the act of doing something good. It is the opposite of maleficence or the act of doing or causing harm. It can, however, feel like maleficence if it is difficult to deliver or you think the person receiving it may be offended.

Psalm 141:5 describes kindness as a blow, a rebuke, or a correction. Kind words are words used to keep us on the straight path. Jesus is the kindest person I know but his words are not nice, sugar-coated, fluffy candyfloss words. His kind words can move mountains, challenge sin, and make blind people see.

Kindness also means we can forgive others. There are two sides to forgiveness. One is the forgiveness that God shows us. The other is the forgiveness we should offer to others. Kindness, compassion and forgiveness are inseparable friends. It is difficult to be kind to someone if we cannot forgive them. But we can learn to forgive because we have been shown compassion from our Father.

Kindness flows from the Spirit

In the second chapter of the second book of Corinthians, the apostle Paul is writing to a church he deeply loves. He is concerned that people within the church are still involved in idol worship or are listening to false prophets. Paul insists that he and his fellow workers have not done or said anything to lead them astray and follow a false gospel.

When Paul laid out his case to the church in Corinth about his leadership, much like a lawyer in a court of law, he did so by describing the challenges he endured for his faith and discussed his spiritual life where God produced spiritual fruit. On that list, kindness is mentioned as a spiritual fruit.[1]

True kindness is produced by God's Spirit in our lives

Galatians 5:22–23 says, 'But the fruit of the Spirit is love, joy, peace, forbearance, kindness, goodness, faithfulness, gentleness and self-control. Against such things there is no law.'

God's Spirit can move the orientation of our hearts towards other people. He can even help us forgive and love people when they are unkind in return. Our aim is to imitate God's kindness by loving our enemies. Our kindness also reflects the tender heart of our Father.

Ephesians 4:32 says, 'Be kind and compassionate to one another, forgiving each other, just as in Christ God forgave you.'

We are told to pursue kindness and God has given his spirit to help us do that:

> Whoever pursues righteousness and kindness will find life, righteousness, and honour.
>
> *Proverbs 21:21*, ESV

Kindness is powerful. It can change you and the person to whom you show kindness.

Practical pointers

Spend some time in God's presence. Ask him to fill and refill you with his Spirit. Ask him to help you grow the fruit of kindness in your life. We are leaky vessels and need to be filled up every day. We need to be connected on a daily basis to the one who fills us.

Summary

Kindness is not a fluffy, sparkly word. It's fearsome. It can yield amazing fruit both in our lives and the lives of those around us.

It can change individual lives. It can change communities.

Look at the story of Ruth. Naomi had survived famine, a move to a different land, and then lost her husband and her sons. Although she tells her friends in Bethlehem that this has made her bitter, it does not stop her from being kind. She shows kindness to her daughters-in-law, releasing them from any obligation to stay with her. And there is Ruth, who shows great kindness towards Naomi by promising to stay with her. She leaves her home and makes a seven-to-ten-day journey to go and live with Naomi, leaving her own family and friends.

Boaz hears of the extraordinary woman called Ruth and he himself responds with great kindness towards her. People's lives are changed by kindness. This is part of God's redeeming plan. Through this kindness Ruth is part of Jesus' genealogy.

We also need to be open to the supernatural work of the Holy Spirit. We need his help; we need his power to grow this fruit in our lives.

Prayer

Thank you, Father, that you first showed us how much you love us.
Help us to be reliant on you and your Spirit.
Make us more like Jesus.
Help us to grow the fruit of your Spirit in our lives.
In Jesus' name.
Amen.

3

The Life of Jesus

Cathy Le Feuvre

So in everything, do to others what you would have them do to you, for this sums up the Law and the Prophets.

Matthew 7:12

Christine Lee is one of the kindest people I know. She's been a great friend to me for years and so I've seen this kindness in action, but she and her husband, Adrian, also live out kindness as Christian leaders in the north of England. Every day, in their mission and ministry in a Salvation Army church and community, they reach out and support and care for marginalised people, including families in crisis, refugees and others perceived to be on the periphery of society. They do this not just because it is their 'job' but because they are impelled by their faith to do so.

However, in turn, the couple have themselves been the recipients of extraordinary kindnesses which helps to motivate their thinking and actions.

Some years ago, Christine was facing a large bill for new spectacles without which she couldn't operate at all – £350 was a large sum so she decided to pay the bill in stages and that's when something extraordinary happened:

> I went to pay my first instalment of £50 and the assistant said that an angel had come in a few days before and paid the bill, in full! To this day I don't know who it was.

As a person of faith, Christine is in no doubt that this was a 'God-incidence':

> It's one of those divine things that happens, and no one gets the credit, just God!

But it was also an example of true human altruism – doing something for another without any thought of recompense, reward or recognition. She told me:

> Kindness encapsulates something that is done for people when you don't expect anything back. So much these days, people want that recognition and even repayment for what they've done, but true kindness is something that is done out of unselfishness and done with so much grace. I think it's not just about the receiver but also the giver. The person who gives the kindness receives so much from it, having done it!

But that wasn't the end of it. In addition, what amazed Christine was not just the impact on herself but also on the staff at the opticians, who were astounded that someone could be so kind. It was a gift that kept on giving!

The matter of the angel and the spectacles wasn't the first time that Christine and Adrian had been on the receiving end of such unadulterated kindness. Years before, when they were struggling financially while Adrian was studying at Bible college, they faced a series of bills amounting to £475, bills which they knew they could not cover with Christine's meagre wages as a part-time music teacher. The pair, as they are wont to do, prayed about it, admitting to God that they had no idea how they were going to pay those four bills. The following day they discovered an envelope on their doormat containing cash to the value of *exactly* £475 – not a pound more or a pound less – and an accompanying note bearing the words: 'I think you need this more than I do'.

Again, the couple never discovered who had sent the money or done this great kindness.

Many people who 'live by faith' have had such experiences of anonymous kindnesses coming out of the blue and to the rescue at just the right time, and Christine believes that faithful living depends on others listening to God and acting upon conviction and extending kindness:

> It means that people have to go with what God is telling them to do. Because if they don't do that kindness, then what was planned will not happen. It's all about the timing as well. When we go with it, God does more than we ask for. He doesn't just answer a prayer, he always goes 'more than . . .'
>
> Things like this are happening every day and sometimes we just don't see them, or we don't recognise them. But I'm convinced that the kindness we see, we will see a lot more of if we recognise that that was God's way of showing us how he loves and cares for us.

Christine and Adrian and many like them do believe that kindness can certainly be God-inspired. This doesn't mean, of course, that non-Christians or people who aren't signed up to faith aren't motivated to do kind things for others. As we'll read later, there's an argument to say that there's something innately kind about all human beings, although of course that can be overwhelmed and ruled out by our selfishness and inability to listen to what we know is the right thing to do.

Kindness – part of God's plan

As people of faith, and particularly for those of us who are Christians, we may wish to consider that kindness is more than just something we do to help others out, whether that's planned or spur-of-the-moment. Our kindness and our actions are, as my friend Christine indicates, part of God's plan, not just for us but for others, including those who might be on the receiving end of our small kindnesses.

If we want inspiration for this type of godly kindness, then we need to look no further than the person of Jesus Christ. We only need to read the first few books of the New Testament and the accounts of his life, to become aware of the sort of kindness he not only shared with those around him but lived out through his very being.

In an online essay, Pamela A. Williams put it like this:

> The Biblical stories of Jesus overflow with acts of kindness. These acts almost read like a language in and of themselves and if we look under a blanket of kindness, we find Jesus speaking love, joy and healing. It is where we find Jesus touching lives and making differences.[1]

I love that idea, that kindness was as natural to Jesus as language and speech. Imagine if all of those who followed him took that example and ran with it. Kindness would become as natural as breathing and thinking, all things we do unconsciously but without which we are not alive! That, I believe, was the nature of Jesus Christ when he walked on this earth and still is his essence today.

Lessons from Jesus' life

There's no doubt from the accounts of his life that Jesus was known to those around him as a pure example of love and kindness, and I have no doubt that those closest to him would have been the recipients of that kindness. A loving look, a smile, a hand stretched out to help in the home, the extra effort put in to ensure that items created in his carpenter's workshop were, perhaps, delivered ahead of schedule.

Of course, there's nothing much in the Bible about Jesus' life before his earthly ministry and mission began at about the age of 30. But we know from the first chapters of the New Testament, which in part tell the narrative of that ministry, that Jesus' life seemed to be infused with kindness. There's no indication that this began when he turned 30. It must have been there before.

But in his kindness, Jesus wasn't just about making others 'feel better', although that obviously is one of the benefits of kindness. He also showed kindness in a different way, to those who others would not interact with. And that, at times, meant a bit of rule-breaking and stepping outside the 'norms' of expected behaviour of the day.

Jesus 'touched' or changed the lives of those around him, but there are also many examples which indicate that the kindness he showed involved actual 'touch', at a time when that was unexpected and even, in some cases, dangerous and culturally inappropriate.

Leprosy is an ancient disease which today is easily treated with a sequence of drugs, but it's still an ailment which results in stigma and disgust, because left untreated or not caught early, it can cause a great deal of deformity and disability. In Jesus' time, and down the centuries, people with leprosy were despised and rejected, often thrown out of their homes, families and social circles because of the fear of infection. Lepers became outcasts and beggars, left to die in the gutter.

Jesus' reputation as a healer was beginning to be widely known, and we read in the Bible that when a man with leprosy approached him and asked to be made clean, Jesus 'reached out his hand and touched the man. "I am willing," he said. "Be clean!" Immediately he was cleansed of leprosy' (Matt. 8:3).

Shocking!

Not just to touch a man with leprosy and put himself in physical jeopardy of contracting the awful disease, but also because to touch such an unclean individual would have made Jesus 'unclean' himself. Ceremonial physical cleanliness connected to spiritual purity was and still is a big deal in Judaism and to deliberately make oneself 'dirty' would have been scandalous.

The result – the miraculous healing of a man with a dreadful debilitating and disfiguring disease – must have blown the minds of those watching, but it showed not only Jesus' awesome power to heal, but his compassion and kindness. It showed he understood human nature and need, and his kindness came from the core of that empathy.

Those with leprosy even today report that one of the issues when suffering from this dreadful disease is not just the physical ailment and even the disability, but the loss of physical contact with another human being. We all need human comfort, hugs and touch, so imagine what it might be like to have been denied that for many years. Yet here comes a man, Jesus, who is happy to touch a leper. The miracle is not just supernatural but intensely human, and it wasn't the only time Jesus showed that physical contact is part of kindliness.

He stretched out his hand to the ill mother-in-law of one of his followers, Peter, helped her up out of bed, and she was well (Mark 1:30–31). In response to the pleas of a widow woman whose only son had just died, Jesus touched the death bier of the recently deceased as he was being carried to his burial and the man was alive again (Luke 7:11–15). Another time, a grieving father, himself a religious leader in the local synagogue, pleaded irrationally for Jesus to bring his little girl back to life. Jesus took the dead girl by the hand and life was miraculously restored (Matt. 9:18–19, 23–25).

How can this be applied today?

On 19 April 1987, Princess Diana, then Princess of Wales, visited the London Middlesex Hospital to open the UK's first unit dedicated to treating people with HIV and AIDS and during that official visit she did something which was not just kind and compassionate, but intentional.

She shook hands with one of the patients, without wearing gloves. That gesture challenged the belief, commonly held at the time but which was and is completely incorrect, that HIV or AIDS could be transmitted by touch.

In that moment, the princess showed that this was a condition which required understanding and compassion, rather than ignorance and fear. It's a moment which has gone down in history, but it wasn't the only time she reached out to those living with the then life-threatening illness. And her actions, her witness to the world, helped to gradually break down the stigma associated with AIDS and to bring about greater understanding. If kindness can do that, what a powerful tool we have at our disposal.

Touch is a very powerful thing. During the COVID-19 pandemic which began in early 2020, many of us have missed hugs and touch. It is a sign of love and compassion, and kindness.

There are still some in our world who are never blessed by the caring touch of others. People who others avoid, for all sorts of reasons. Homeless people, those living on the margins of society. I know of one outreach worker who at one time washed the feet of those homeless people she and others fed on a regular basis. To touch a person who no one else will go near is not just a kindness, but a Jesus thing to do!

The great thing about Jesus, though, is that he didn't need to even reach out a hand to touch a person to change their lives. He did this just by being who he was.

Zacchaeus

Zacchaeus was a nasty piece of work. As a chief tax collector in the town of Jericho, he was despised. He was a Jew but was working for the Roman authorities so he would have been considered by many as a 'traitor'. In addition, tax collectors were often notorious for being corrupt, creaming off cash for themselves before submitting the monies gathered from his community to the powers-that-be.

He wanted to meet Jesus, although we're not really told why – maybe he was having a bit of a crisis of conscience. But his encounter with Jesus was life-changing. Jesus saw him in a tree while he was walking through a crowd, called him down, and then went to his house for a meal (Luke 19:1–10).

Can you imagine the conversation? Maybe Jesus questioned him about his ethics and morals? Or perhaps by just being in his presence, Zacchaeus realised the error of his ways and changed his life around, becoming a generous person who determined to give away half of all he had. And not just that, as his story in the New Testament tells us:

> Zacchaeus stood up and said to the Lord, 'Look, Lord! Here and now I give half of my possessions to the poor, and if I have cheated anybody out of anything, I will pay back four times the amount.'
>
> *Luke 19:8*

Having Jesus step over the threshold of Zacchaeus' house and sit down to eat and drink with him would have been a very powerful and outrageous statement, not just to the man himself but also to the community. Jesus was, by this time, gaining a reputation as a 'rabbi' or teacher and one who healed and did great acts of kindness. But to extend the hand of friendship and kindness to someone who was so hated and excluded by his fellow Jews would have sent a strong message. No one is beyond the pale! Everyone is worthy of kindness!

Again, Jesus steps out of the conventions of his time to show not just kindness, but the essence of who he was; showing that even those who are considered to have damaged society, or are the cause of unrest and discontent, or even those who sow seeds of hatred and conflict are to be treated with kindness, as we would those of whom we approve and agree. No one is excluded in Jesus' world.

The kindness of Jesus was and is a physical thing, but it goes further than that. He came not just to show us the example of how to live, but to save and bring people into his fold. The story of Zacchaeus ends like this:

> Jesus said to him, 'Today salvation has come to this house, because this man, too, is a son of Abraham. For the Son of Man came to seek and to save the lost.'
>
> *Luke 19:9–10*

So here we come to another interesting point about the kindliness that Jesus displayed and which we are called to emulate.

Just because he was kind, doesn't mean he was a pushover!

The way that Jesus interacted with Zacchaeus was certainly done with kindness and compassion, friendliness and consideration and generosity of spirit. Note that he didn't berate the tax collector for his misdemeanours in front of the crowd but instead went quietly with him to his house where they sat down together and ate and drank. It was only then that the *big* conversation about Zacchaeus' life, behaviour, motives and values began.

Undoubtedly the truth that Jesus spoke made the man squirm, and I'm sure the challenges must have been delivered with a certain voracity and firmness. He challenged Zacchaeus, but he must have made the message palatable, because we read that the tax collector 'repented' and promised to change his ways. That sort of kindness, delivered with compassion but also strength and confidence, is what we're seeing here.

Is being kind just about being 'nice'?

We have already looked at the difference between being kind and being 'nice', but let's look at this a bit more.

In the introduction to his book *Love Kindness: Discover the Power of a Forgotten Christian Virtue*,[2] Professor Barry H. Corey makes a significant distinction between 'kindness' and 'niceness'.

Now I'm *sure* Jesus was civil and polite (and yes, 'nice') even when he was being strong and persistent. But Professor Corey notes that 'being nice' is different to 'being kind': 'Kindness is certainly not aggression, but it's also not niceness. Niceness is cosmetic. It's bland . . . Kindness is fierce, never to be mistaken for niceness. They're not the same and never were. Kindness is neither timid not frail, as niceness can be so easily.'[3]

Professor Corey, whose book is really a discourse on kindness and a call to 'live and love the forgotten way of kindness', emphasises the need to make the distinction between being truly kind as Jesus was and is, and rather dull 'niceness'.

He reminds us that right from the start of Christianity, Jesus' followers have 'walked the risky and sometimes dangerous road of kindness', and that actually gives me some encouragement – I'm not the first person to struggle with all this.

But he also points out that today's 'polarised culture' means that often people become very fixed in their opinions, or terribly relaxed and seemingly 'soft', and that can cause conflict and make things very tricky for those of us trying to live differently, perhaps counter culturally. Professor Corey challenges us to live in an alternative way, what he calls 'a third way' – one where we discard the extremes of 'firm centres and hard edges' and 'the weakness of spongy centres and soft edges' and instead start simply . . . with kindness.

I don't know about you but I don't want to be seen as a pushover and weak, or as someone so intransigent that I can't see any other opinions or way forward but my own. Maybe we can, as Professor Corey says, embrace the sort of kindness that is '. . . the way of firm centres and soft edges.' We might need some help, so where better to look than the life of Jesus?

Back to Zacchaeus. He must have been a tough cookie to survive in the tax collector world of the first century AD. He had to deal with the Roman and other authorities and he lived with the scorn and rejection of his fellow Jews. I often surmise that he would have been rather cold-hearted, selfish and immune to criticism.

So how did Jesus get through to him? Certainly, I guess, not just by saying in a rather twee voice, 'Come on, Zacchaeus, time to mend your ways.' There must have been something more about Jesus which was compelling, because his conversation over that meal with the tax collector struck to the core of the man and made him turn his life around.

None of this of course, is in the Bible narrative, but I think that's the nature of Jesus' kindness. He didn't go around being 'nice' just because he could, or even doing acts of random kindness so he could feel good about himself and make others feel good too. He was more intentional and he had a deeper purpose – to reveal who God is and the extent of his love for the world, to show love and share love and to bring people to him, so that we might also have that same spirit.

He challenges, as well as smiles. He questions, but not in a threatening fashion. He intervenes in arguments and pours peace into situations that could get out of hand. He steps outside the conventions of his day, and is not afraid to defy what the world thinks is 'correct' or acceptable behaviour. He's courageous, putting himself in danger – not just physical danger but also in the line of fire for criticism.

If we are to be Jesus followers, then we need to consider that *this* is the sort of kindness we should be embracing.

The verse with which this chapter began says this: 'So in everything, do to others what you would have them do to you, for this sums up the Law and the Prophets' (Matt. 7:12).

These are words spoken by Jesus in what has become known as the 'Sermon on the Mount'. It's got some life-changing challenges for us. Ask and you shall receive, don't judge or you'll be judged, don't be a hypocrite, give to the poor, don't worry about things you can't control, be salt and light to the world . . . be different! And that sermon also teaches us how to pray because it includes what is now known as 'The Lord's Prayer' (Matt. 6:9–13).

Much of what Jesus was saying was radical but this instruction – do to others as you would have them do to you – might have been a bit more familiar to his listeners. It's what has subsequently been dubbed the 'Golden Rule' and it's a way of being and acting which crosses culture, religions and time.

In Jersey in the Channel Islands there's an organisation called Kindness Connects. Its founder, Brian Clarke, has organised and hosted four Kindness Festivals – in 2015, 2017, 2019 and 2021 – which bring together people who share kindness every day through their work; small charities which may not get a lot of publicity ordinarily share what they do with the public. It's always a brilliant day, with much love being shared on the harbourside in a village called St Aubin, and it's always defined by a real spirit of cooperation, friendliness and yes . . . kindness.

For Brian, kindness is something tangible and he explained that Kindness Connects takes its theme from the Golden Rule, or the ethic of reciprocity:

> This is wisdom in action, and you will find it in the writing of every established religion, including both those that are God-given and secular.

The call to kindness in other religious approaches

From one of the oldest continuously practised religions, Zoroastrianism – 'Do not do unto others whatever is injurious to yourself'[4] – to one of the world's 'newest' religions, the Bahá'í faith: 'Lay not on any soul a load that you would not wish to be laid upon you, and desire not for anyone the things you would not desire for yourself.'[5]

From Buddhism – 'Treat not others in ways that you yourself would find hurtful'[6] to Confucianism: 'One phrase which sums up the basis of all good conduct . . . *loving kindness*: do not do to others what you do not want done to yourself'[7] to

Hinduism: 'This is the sum of duty: do not do to others what would cause pain if done to you.'[8] and Islam – 'None of you [truly] believes until he wishes for his brother what he wishes for himself'[9] – this sentiment appears to be a 'golden rule' of humanity.

It appears in the teachings of most spiritual philosophies and religions, from Ancient Egypt to indigenous American spirituality, the Roman pagan religion, Shinto, Sikhism, Sufism, Taoism, Unitarianism, and ancient wisdom from the Yoruba tribe in Nigeria. And if we think this is just motivated by faith, that's not the case. The principle of doing unto others is also embraced by those who would lay no claim to faith at all. Humanism also recognises what is known as the Golden Rule and various writings explain that this means that '. . . people should aim to treat each other as they would like to be treated themselves – with tolerance, consideration and compassion.'[10]

As a Jew, Jesus would have been familiar with the Judaic teaching which says this: 'What is hateful to you, do not do to your neighbour: this is the whole Torah – all the rest is commentary.'[11] And those listening to his Sermon on the Mount would have known all about that too.

Although it's never referred to in the Bible as the 'Golden Rule', the exhortation pops up from time to time. Take the moment that a group of religious leaders, the Pharisees, wanted to catch Jesus out. They asked him this question:

> 'Teacher, which is the greatest commandment in the Law?' Jesus replied: '"Love the Lord your God with all your heart and with all your soul and with all your mind." This is the first and greatest commandment. And the second is like it: "Love your neighbour as yourself." All the Law and the Prophets hang on these two commandments.'
>
> *Matthew 22:36–40*

For Jesus it's not just about duty, or even following religious or cultural rules. It's not just about doing good to others so that people don't treat you badly in the future. It's more profound than that. It's loving others like we love ourselves. Now, that's a challenge, especially if we don't like ourselves very much and are unkind to ourselves.

This way of living like Jesus may not be easy to understand and follow through on; that kindness where we may need to put ourselves in another person's shoes before we act, or to put aside our own needs before that of another, or where we maybe need to stand up and be brave when we see wrong being done. This may need a change of perception, ambition and heart. We may need to change our own motivations. It may be a life's journey.

It's the sort of Jesus-like kindness which is not just 'nice' because we don't want to upset people and don't want to be thought of badly, rather it's a strong and courageous kindness, changing the world around us from the inside out and yet doing it with compassion, without anger, without conflict. Now, that could be tough!

There's a concept which many advocate when thinking about how we can begin to live this life with Jesus' kindness. When we face challenges, or we're going into difficult situations, we might want to ask ourselves . . . 'What would Jesus do?'

Sounds simple? Lots of us down the years have worn those 'WWJD' bracelets as a constant reminder of the life lived by Jesus which we aim to imitate.

It's a concept which has roots deep in ancient and Christian theology. Down the centuries people have considered the question as a form of *imitatio dei*, the 'imitation of God'. It was part of some ancient religions and philosophies, but in Christianity, especially in Eastern Orthodox and Roman Catholicism, it gained traction as believers were encouraged to take on the character of God, a process called *theosis* in Greek. This doctrine derives from the biblical mandate to be holy as God is holy (Lev. 20:26).

What would Jesus do?

It's not a doctrine that was originally widely embraced by Protestantism or evangelical Christianity, but back at the end of the nineteenth century, a bestselling book articulated the theological concept for a new audience.

The Revd Charles Monroe Sheldon was an American Congregational minister who in the winter of 1896 began preaching a series of 'sermon stories' to his congregation at the Central Congregational Church in Topeka, Kansas in which he asked the question 'What would Jesus do?'

He brought together his stories and his thinking in a novel entitled *In His Steps*, published in 1896[12] which ultimately posed some crucial questions: 'What would his congregants and his readers do when faced with moral and ethical decisions? What difference does our faith make to the world we live in?'

For Revd Sheldon, the idea of 'What Would Jesus Do?' wasn't just something 'nice' to do . . . it actually went to the heart of his Christian faith. He was an advocate of a late nineteenth-century school of thought known as Christian Socialism, and he became a leader of the Social Gospel movement, a social movement within Protestantism that sought to apply Christian ethics to the social problems of the day, and issues relating to social justice like poverty, economic inequality, crime, racial tension, child labour, addictions and even the lack of unionisation and the dangers of war.

The 'What Would Jesus Do?' approach to Christian theology became very popular at the turn of the twentieth century, and as many of us know, if we wore those bracelets, it also gained popularity about a century later. Since it was first published, Revd Sheldon's *In His Steps* is reckoned to have sold more than 50 million copies. He followed it up with a sequel called *Jesus is Here*[13] which was set a few years after the first book and in which Christ actually shows up and visits the characters who featured in the first book.

Imagine that! Not just a bracelet to remind us to constantly ask 'What Would Jesus Do?' but the man himself, showing us the way to live!

If we're honest with ourselves, and I hope we are, sometimes that WWJD bracelet, homemade with twine and beads in a craft session at church or at camp, became a fashion accessory. Am I right? Discovering what Jesus did in given circumstances which were thrown at him and discerning what that might mean for our own behaviour, is much more challenging.

Can we live the Jesus way?

If we met a Zacchaeus, could we put aside our natural inclination to criticise and condemn but rather just listen, challenge kindly, encourage them to think about their future, and to embrace them as a neighbour and friend? Even if we got criticism for doing so?

If we see a homeless person on the street, maybe behaving irrationally and smelling rather pungent and swearing through the alcohol and drug addiction, can we treat them with compassion as a friend, washing their feet as Jesus washed the feet of his disciples, putting our arms around their shoulders?

Can we set aside our desire to promote our own agendas, even through our so-called 'kindliness' and 'acts of kindness'? Can we be like my friend Christine's anonymous 'angel' – helping another with no thought of reward or recognition? Just being, as Christine said, the vehicle for '. . . one of those divine things that happens, and where no one gets the credit, just God!'

If we see social injustice and inequalities, are we prepared to stand up for what we think is right? Without ranting, or even drawing attention to ourselves, but just because it is the kind and right thing to do? Can we be kind and courageous in equal measure, as Jesus was? Can we be, in this respect and many others, the hands and feet and voice and spirit of Jesus in our own time and place?

Well, the good news is that we're not alone in our efforts. First, we have the life of Jesus as an example – loving family member, friend, teacher, healer, challenger, kindly intervener in times of turmoil. And we are blessed with other scriptures to encourage and guide us. I'm not the first to say it, but I believe kindness is a biblical way of thinking. It even makes the shortlist of the 'fruits of the Spirit' found in Galatians 5 where Paul reminds us that it's not an optional choice, but the result of having the Holy Spirit fill us and live through us (v. 22).

Professor Barry Corey says it better than I can: 'We exhale kindness after we inhale what's been breathed into us by the Spirit. Kindness radiates when we're earnest about living the way of Christ, the way of the Spirit. Kindness displays the wonder of Christ's love through us.'[14]

Practical pointers

A simple yet profound action would be to try to live life constantly asking ourselves that question, 'What would Jesus do?'

Next time we are faced with a situation where we would naturally run away, or criticise, let's stop ourselves and think, 'What might Jesus do right now?'

When we see opportunities for kindness, let's not hang back and wonder if it's the 'right' thing to do. Remember what Jesus did and get stuck in.

Summary

The life of Jesus overflows with kindness. He stretched out his hands to help others, including many who were ostracised and despised. He challenged the cultural norms of his day to include and bless not just those who he liked and who were like him, but also those who were considered different.

But being kind is not always the easy option. Being kind is not just 'being nice' so that we won't offend people and people will like us, or because we want something in return. Sometimes kindness may require courage as we dare to defy conventions and step out in faith to change our world and to help right wrongs. It may sometimes mean putting the needs of others before our own, and understanding that through showing kindness we are not only learning more about the nature of Jesus Christ, but that our kindness and actions are part of a bigger plan, God's plan, not just for us but for others, including those who might be on the receiving end of our small kindnesses.

Prayer

Jesus,

Thank you for the example of kindness that you showed during your time on earth.

Thank you for all the lessons you teach, in words and actions, and for understanding that we have a very long way to go before we can get anywhere close to being as kind as you.

Inspire us to constantly remember to treat others as our neighbour, not just because it's what we are called to do, but because we are living a life that is kindness to the core.

We pray for open doors to opportunities to share kindness. For conversations and meetings where it's obvious that a kind action is required and for courage and discernment to determine what we need to do, not just to make a difference to another life but to make a difference in our world.

In the name of Jesus we pray.

Amen.

4

The Science of Kindness

Debbie Duncan

Kindness is the language which the deaf can hear and the blind can see.

Unknown[1]

Did you know that there is a science to kindness – that there are scientifically proven benefits to being kind? There are journal articles written about kindness, whole textbooks devoted to the subject, it is taught at the most prestigious institutions. I think it's amazing.

As Christians we try to be kind, knowing that God showed us great kindness before we even knew his name. We respond by trying to live as Jesus would live. His Spirit helps us to show kindness even to our enemies. What we don't realise is that being kind actually has a physiological impact on our own bodies.

Kindness has been shown to increase physical and mental wellbeing. The medical psychotherapists Ballatt and Campling in their 2011 research study show that in altruistic individuals, increased activity in the posterior superior temporal cortex of the brain has been reported.[2] This means that individual acts of kindness lead to a release of the particular hormones which have a positive effect on our bodies. Kindness also impacts our psychological wellbeing. Participants who had a magnetic imaging (MRI) scan of their brains showed that even the act of thinking of compassion and kindness activates the emotional regulation system of the brain.[3]

The physical benefits of kindness

When someone is kind or they themselves receive kindness, there's a positive effect on the body. It is strange to say, but acts of kindness give our 'love hormone' levels a boost.

It makes me think of the period dramas that I love. In many of the novels the heroine falls deeply in love with the man who shows her a modicum of kindness! What actually happens is that as our subconscious mind is deciding that we like someone, the chemical messengers in our brain are sending us all sorts of messages. One such neurotransmitter or chemical messenger is oxytocin, which is sometimes called the 'love hormone', as it plays a role in forming social bonds and enabling us to trust people. It's also the hormone mothers produce when they breastfeed, cementing their bond with their babies. Oxytocin is released when we're physically intimate with someone, too. It's tied to making us more trusting, more generous, and friendlier, while also lowering our blood pressure. It is, in fact, also called 'liquid trust'.

There is a lot of research being done at the moment looking at oxytocin and its role in empathy. What we know is that it impacts social emotions and behaviours such as trust, empathy, cooperation, social attention, eye gaze, as well as a response to psychosocial stress.[4] Actually, just thinking about or witnessing acts of kindness produces an increase in oxytocin levels. Oxytocin increases our self-esteem and optimism. It also lowers blood pressure and improves our cardiac health.

I think it is uncomfortable for us to talk about key topics like love and trust as a result of chemicals and liquid proteins, but I want to remind us that this is only part of the story. Oxytocin makes us more trusting but doesn't make us trust. It makes us more sympathetic to another person but does not make us love them. I think if that was the case, we would have a real-life love potion on our hands, or it could have the potential to be exploited by armies and politicians. Thankfully this is still science fiction, although in one research study in 2015 of men and women given oxytocin, their compassion levels rose, though it was only increased towards women. Oxytocin did not increase compassion towards men.[5] Their conclusion was that there was an evolutionary component increasing compassion to those who are deemed the vulnerable and caregivers in society. It does show that you cannot use it to manipulate whole communities. That's a relief!

Dr W.W. IsHak, a professor of psychiatry at Cedars-Sinai Hospital in Los Angeles, suggests that acts of random kindness lead to the releasing of the chemical dopamine which can give us a feeling of euphoria.[6] Dopamine is the feel-good brain chemical. It is released when we are expecting a reward, or when someone is kind to us, and makes us happy. Nicotine from cigarettes and alcohol can also activate the dopamine cycle, increasing their addictive qualities.

In addition to boosting oxytocin and dopamine, being kind can also increase serotonin, a neurotransmitter that helps regulate mood. Serotonin is called a monoamine neurotransmitter and it's one of the widely distributed neurochemicals in the human nervous system. Neurochemicals are really the body's chemical messengers. They are often used to pass messages from the nerves to muscles or nerves to nerves. One which you may have heard of is noradrenaline, which works in the body to control blood pressure and heart rate, as well as many other functions.

It is difficult to identify the main function of serotonin, but it is more concentrated in certain structures of the brain than other areas. It is found to be in high amounts in the medial orbitofrontal cortex, which is considered to be the 'social brain' – the area of the brain responsible for social cognition and decision-making.[7] Serotonin is associated with cooperation and affiliation, and reacts to antisocial behaviours such as aggression and social isolation.

We all have moral codes that dictate how people should treat one another, how we care for others and prevent harm. They also relate to the fair distribution of resources and positive social interactions. It is this sense of justice that is thought to be a central building block in our moral codes across cultures. Serotonin increases our concerns for justice and fairness. If we are kind, serotonin levels increase and so does our ability to be just and fair. It's a justice hormone – I think that's so cool! Despite some understanding of its effects, the neurobiological and psychological mechanisms involved in this process are unclear. I think that's a good thing as there is the potential for neuroscientists to use them to shape our social behaviour and even manipulate our ethical values. This all sounds like a Hollywood movie, doesn't it?

We can already see how people's behaviour is altered by different categories of drugs that are commonly used in the NHS. As a nurse working in primary care, I commonly cared for people with a problem with their mental health. In fact, it is thought that one in four patients attend their GP practice with a problem with their mental health. It may even be as high as one in three. One of the medications that we use to help people who suffer anxiety and depression is called citalopram. It's been very successful in helping people recover from a fracture in their mental health. It is from a class of drugs called selective serotonin reuptake inhibitors (SSRI). It works by increasing the amount of serotonin in the brain to restore a sense of balance and equilibrium. I have seen it help many people. There is definitely a place for these drugs and some of you reading this may be prescribed them. I am a firm believer in relying on God for his healing hands in our lives and utilising everything that he has given.

Luke, who wrote one of the gospels and the book of Acts, was a doctor; he worked with Paul to spread the news of Jesus far and wide. I love the fact that God put a medic on the team of the first Christians! Why did I say all that? It is because being kind helps to release serotonin within our bodies and this helps us to maintain mental stability and often an elevated mood. Being kind simply leads to us feeling good about ourselves and keeps us happy! Studies have also found that people are significantly less likely to behave in a self-interested manner or act selfishly if they have higher levels of serotonin.[8]

Psychological benefits

Kindness seems to be a hot topic in psychology, particularly during the COVID-19 pandemic. If you are a kind person then you are considered a good teacher, nurse or boss. It is something that is viewed as a positive attribute in those around us. It alters the brain, improves our mood and it reduces our blood pressure by reducing the hormone cortisol. It can reduce our risk of developing type 2 diabetes and cardiovascular disease. Kindness can even improve our body's immunity to infection and lead to longer life.

It can make you feel satisfied with life because of the release of serotonin and dopamine. Kindness can reduce anxiety and depression. It even acts as a painkiller – as you are kind or people are kind to you, you produce endorphins which are the body's natural painkillers. It can reduce loneliness, help build relationships and strengthen communities. And just like an infectious disease, it is also contagious.

Kindness is considered to be a behavioural action that others can see. It is characterised by the qualities of affection and warmth. Sometimes it is confused with compassion, which relates more to the qualities of sympathy, empathy and concern.

Compassion

It is thought that there are three requirements for compassion to occur. These are:

1. Something that evokes our feelings.
2. The sufferers' troubles are a result of an unjust fate.
3. We must be able to picture ourselves in the same predicament.[9]

Compassion, as well as kindness, is related to increased happiness and a greater sense of mental wellbeing. Compassion in medicine is related to better patient satisfaction and even improved outcomes. And just like kindness, it is also associated with improved health for those delivering it.

The study of kindness

The study of kindness is researched using two approaches to experiments in psychology. These are 'prosocial spending' and 'acts of kindness'. In prosocial spending experiments, participants are given money and offered the opportunity to donate it to, or buy something for, others. In acts of kindness experiments, participants are typically instructed to perform kind behaviours towards other people over the course of the study.

Certainly, spending money on others or prosocial spending leads to a greater momentary happiness than spending money on oneself. In one study,[10] 1,712 students were asked to purchase something for themselves or a stranger in need. Those who spent their money on the stranger were happier. It certainly explains why so many people give to charity.

It amazes me each year when I see the totals raised for events like the BBC's *Children in Need*. In 2020, *Children in Need* raised £37m which grew to £57m during the subsequent months. The average person in Britain gives at least £10 a month to charity. Although many feel they are doing it because of a sense of duty – giving back to society – for many it is because it makes them feel good.

In an article in *The Guardian* in 2015, Michael Sanders and Francesca Tamma looked at the topic 'the science behind why people give money to charity'.[11] They found that giving is contagious, because seeing or hearing about others giving money to charity makes us want to do the same. They also found that spending money on others, being kind, makes us feel good about ourselves. It actually makes us happy!

The prosocial spending experiments showed that the happiness was momentary. In Gill Hasson's book *Kindness*, she highlights a study done by a University of Pennsylvania team headed by Dr Martin Seligman.[12] They asked the participants in the study to write a thank you letter to someone they had always meant to thank but hadn't got time to do it. After they finished the task, they were asked to complete a happiness score. It was raised and the participants found this lasted for about a month after the event.

Several years ago, I realised that there were a few people in my life that I wanted to thank. These were people who had taught me about Jesus and helped me grow to know him. One was the minister of the first church I went to as a teenager. He was called Revd Grant Bell. He had been seriously ill, and I knew he was in the last days of his life. I wrote him a letter thanking him for his impact on my life. The other person I wanted to thank was a lovely lady who had worked on the mission field for many years. She used to write to me and I to her. I knew she faithfully prayed for my family. I had been told she had passed away several years before and I was disappointed I had left it too late.

I flew up to Scotland and attended the funeral of Revd Bell. While I was there, an elderly lady came over and chatted to me for a while. I knew I should know her but could not remember who she was. I realised that I probably had not met some of the people who were at the funeral for about twenty years. I managed to ask a friend and was told who this lady was. It was the lady who had been the missionary in Africa; she hadn't died all those years before. I texted my husband, 'Funeral went well. One buried and one raised from the dead'. God had given me a chance to say thank you. I was so thrilled. I was happy for months after and have kept in touch ever since. Sometimes a few words of thanks can be life-changing.

I think being kind means that we focus on the world around us more. It takes us out of ourselves and our own circumstances. When we focus on ourselves, our world becomes very small, but when we are kind and focus on others, our world expands. It also has to be intentional. The other important point is that the more we practise it, the better we get at being kind. I think this is especially true during challenging times. Kindness becomes our habitual reaction in whatever circumstances we find ourselves in. I think we also try to be creative about how we can deliver kindness.

What is intelligent kindness?

Intelligent kindness is considered to be a creative, problem-solving, inspiring form of kindness that is more challenging than the usual kindness we are aware of. It is used a lot in healthcare because the more this is utilised, the more trust is developed between the patient and their carer. The relationship becomes a therapeutic one with positive outcomes for both. It can also be defined as compassion. In nursing, this is how care is delivered through relationships and is based on empathy, respect and dignity.

A lot of focus on intelligent kindness has been written about in medical and psychology literature following the Francis Report which looked at the serious failings of the Mid Staffordshire NHS Foundation Trust. A public enquiry took place and the report was published in 2010.

The Mid Staffordshire Trust had allowed the following to happen: 'Patients were left in excrement in soiled bed clothes for lengthy periods' and 'Water was left out of reach'.[13]

Robert Francis observed: 'Staff treated patients and those close to them with what appeared to be callous indifference.' He also wrote: 'Patients must be the first priority in all of what the NHS does . . . [and] receive effective care from caring, compassionate and committed staff, working within a common culture.'[14]

This was a terrible indictment of what happens when we lose sight of the importance of kindness within the nursing profession. Many of the reports that followed this enquiry suggested that there needed to be an urgent shift in the culture of the NHS and that there was a case for a conscious focus or intentional action of intelligent kindness.[15] Some of the literature also suggested that there needed to be a link between compassionate practice, affecting patient experience and linking to staff morale, effectiveness, efficiency and outcome. We need to deliver compassionate care that extends from our philosophy and moral code.[16] Certainly, the culture in nursing has now changed, with compassion and kindness central to nursing practice. The values associated with this compassionate care are: care at the core of what nurses do, compassion, courage to do the right thing, communication, competence and commitment. These are values nurses are encouraged to learn and cultivate in their own lives and nursing practice.

Intelligent kindness is also linked with reform of the social welfare system and is a case for sociological engagement with kindness. We are more aware as a society of the physical and psychological benefits of kindness and are looking at how we can weave it through our communities. I often think this is the type of community our faith communities should be. The problem is that it can be made up of flawed people. The good news is that we can ask God to help us be kinder people. Imagine what that would look like. We have a blueprint of that in Acts 2:44–47:

> All the believers were together and had everything in common. They sold property and possessions to give to anyone who had need. Every day they continued to meet together in the temple courts. They broke bread in their homes and ate together with glad and sincere hearts, praising God and enjoying the favour of all the people. And the Lord added to their number daily those who were being saved.

So, if we know that kindness is something we can cultivate in our lives, we need to think of the things that help it grow. Other people's kindness can change us, and we too can change through implementing the simplest of actions. Our behaviour can change. We can also ask God to enable his Spirit to help us grow the fruit of kindness in our lives.

Practical pointers

How to start developing a kind life:

- We need to be able to recognise kindness.
- We need to change our stance. If we realise we are having a bad day, we should be intentional and decide to make it better for other people.
- Sometimes we just need to STOP. 'S' stands for stop. 'T' stands for take a breath. 'O' for observe. What is happening around us? Maybe we need to act. Then, finally, 'P' is for practise responding, rather than reacting to people or a situation.
- We should focus on kindness. This may mean we want to meditate and ruminate on what it is and how we can be a kinder person; incline our mind towards kindness.

Summary

There is no doubt that being kind to someone will often make their day. When I was out and about doing errands today, I decided to be really intentional in my interactions with people in the shops I visited. I do try to be kind, but today I really tried to *ensure* I was kind. I remember coming back with a little buzz in my steps. I think they had a brighter day and I know that I had a better day.

Prayer
Jesus,
We cannot express how much we owe you.
You gave your life to us.
Giving our life to you and your purposes is what we want to do.
Lord, help us to be like you.
Father, help us to exhibit the qualities of your Son.
We do not care if there are benefits for us from living this way.
We want to live our lives in gratitude for what you have done for us.
In Jesus' name.
Amen.

5

The Impact of Kindness on the Individual

Debbie Duncan

Treat everyone with politeness, even those who are rude to you – not because they are nice, but because you are.

Unknown

We know from the last chapter that being kind and receiving kindness can have a physiological and psychological effect on us. In this chapter we are going to focus on how kindness impacts us as an individual. That is how kindness can impact the whole person – our body, soul and mind.

We can probably all remember an occurence when people have been kind to us. Only a few weeks ago, I found an apple pie sitting at my front door with a tub of whipped cream. I must confess it is one of my favourite things! It made me smile. Every time I thought about it, I smiled. I had no idea who had made it. It was delicious. The flavour of the apple pie and the kindness of the person stayed with me all day.

Kindness can impact your physical, mental and spiritual health. We were nourished physically by that gift. Acts of kindness also cause a rise in our endorphins, oxytocin and serotonin. We are reminded of other gifts of kindness. Not only does kindness lift the spirit but it can also increase our self-esteem. We feel like someone cares about us. Someone cared about me enough to bake an apple pie, whip some cream, and leave it on my doorstep. These random acts can even impact the way we think about ourselves.

Self-esteem

Self-esteem is our subjective view or evaluation of what we think we are worth. It encompasses the belief we have about ourselves. I know that God loves me, but some days I don't feel like he does and I may even believe that I am not worthy. Our self-esteem is impacted by positive and negative ideas and beliefs. It can also be affected by our early life experiences. If we are brought up in a home where we are not shown love, then we grow up with low self-esteem, believing that we are unloved. It is a mix of our internal confidence and what we consider as our external achievements. Positive self-esteem can lead to happiness, job and relationship satisfaction.

Interestingly, the idea or concept of self-esteem was first introduced to our thinking by the eighteenth-century Scottish philosopher David Hume (1711–76). He suggested that having a positive value to how we think about ourselves enables us to reach our full potential. The problem with that philosophy is that it must be grounded. An inflated self-esteem and ego based on a faulty construct can lead to ideas of grandeur and/or have a negative effect on those around us. We have all met those people who have an inflated self-esteem.

As a Christian I have learned that my own self-esteem needs to be grounded in what God says about me. My personal self-esteem is flawed.

- God says I am loved
- God says I am chosen

- God says I am his treasure
- God says I am the apple of his eye
- He knows every hair on my head
- He knew me from when I was conceived[1]

Possibly a healthier alternative to self-esteem is self-acceptance. Those who have a healthy self-esteem are found to accept and love themselves unconditionally. They accept their flaws and still love themselves. I think this sits better with a biblical framework of the world. Jesus teaches us to love ourselves because he first loved us (1 John 4:19). We know we are broken, flawed people, yet he died for us. It is from that understanding of ourselves that we can love other people.

> 'Love the Lord your God with all your heart and with all your soul and with all your mind and with all your strength.' The second is this: 'Love your neighbour as yourself.'
>
> *Mark 12:30–31*

Psychology views self-esteem as a measurable aspect of how we see ourselves. This is important if we want to consider how kindness impacts the individual. We must have a way to measure it.

There are two key components of self-esteem – *self-image* and *self-confidence.*

Self-image is the idea we have of our own talents and abilities, character and personality. It is the true reflection we have of ourselves. To have positive self-esteem we need to have a true self-image which mirrors what others say of us. We also need to be self-confident, which is based on a belief that one's efforts and abilities will allow one to reach a goal. It is the ability to take charge of our own life or destiny.

Self-image is how we see ourselves in relation to the world. It is not, however, a true reflection of how God sees us. Sometimes the truth is hidden by wrong ideas and self-beliefs, like thick make-up caked on a face so we don't see a person's true natural beauty.

Self-image therefore answers the following questions:

- What do you think you look like physically?
- What kind of person do you think you are, which includes your beliefs and personal values?
- What do you think others think of you?
- What do you believe are your personal traits such as your strengths and weaknesses?
- How much do you like yourself?

Sometimes in an aim to measure self-esteem and self-confidence we also need to consider self-efficacy, which is a person's belief that they can achieve a specific goal or task. Confusing, isn't it? But that is because these things can be hard to measure. There are scales that can help research this information such as the Rosenberg Self-Esteem Scale or the General Self-Efficacy Scale which allocates marks to statements such as 'I feel I have a number of good qualities' or 'I am a failure'. It's helpful to know that there are objective tests that are used to measure something which can appear very subjective. They validate the research and show us the significance of the findings.

Kindness can have a positive impact on our self-esteem, our self-efficacy and self-confidence. In one large American study in 2017 published in a psychology journal, researchers examined the impact of kindness displayed by prosocial behaviour from 681 young people to strangers.[2] They found that this act of kindness improved the participants' self-esteem. They felt good about themselves. They also examined their actions towards friends and family, and the results were less obvious. Interestingly, just learning about kindness in a high school setting also has this positive effect on students' self-esteem and social self-efficacy.[3]

I think this is a good reason for including teaching about kindness in our school and young adult's curriculums. During early years we can focus too much on personal development. These studies show that having a wider world view, focusing on others and being kind helps our young people to develop and grow into confident people. Certainly, kindness has been a key topic in most educational curriculums in recent years.

Kindness not only leads to an increase in self-esteem in young people within an educational setting but it can also impact people of all age groups. It's probably worth mentioning here that kindness also means different things to different people. It can be dependent on age, ethnicity and their social background. If you are trying to practise kindness, then find out what small act of kindness will mean more to the person you are trying to bless. They may appreciate you spending time with them, or a homemade apple pie.

Interestingly, in an article by Sarah M. Tashjian (based at the Californian Institute of Technology) and fellow researchers published in the journal on cognitive, affective and behavioural neuroscience, they suggested that people with less money often showed more generosity, charitability, and helpfulness than others.[4] I have met kind people of all ages, ethnicity and social backgrounds.

The difference is not about age or social class, but because of emotional intelligence or a societal awareness. This can even be seen in young children who are brought up in a home where they are encouraged to discuss issues around need and want.

They seem to be more intuitive to people in need. The more aware we are of our world around us, the quicker we will respond with kindness.

Self-compassion

In November 2014, my nephew died suddenly in tragic circumstances. It was the start of a two-year period when our family went through the extremes of pain and loss; we lost six close members of my husband's family – three of which were through suicide. No one could have prepared us for the trauma of those years. One counsellor suggested that the closest event would be losing several members of your family in a car crash all at the same time. As a family we learned many lessons. We knew we were carried by the prayers of family, friends and strangers. We were impacted by their great kindness and compassion.

After my brother-in-law's sudden death in April 2014, I ended up in hospital the next day with a pulmonary embolism – seriously ill. We had just signed the paperwork to buy a house in Northern Ireland. At the time we were living in the south of England. We had four grownup children and they all needed somewhere to stay. My husband asked for help. Within twenty-four hours the new house was kitted out with everything we needed from beds and bedding to a microwave and crockery. I remember sitting in hospital receiving messages from the family telling me of the amazing help we had been given. I felt loved and uplifted by the kindness of strangers. I also learned to be kind to myself. I think this is one of the lessons that has stayed with me. To travel the deepest valleys, we need to have self-compassion. We need to be kind to ourselves. If we don't, the journey is much harder, longer and feels like a dark place.

Having this self-compassion is no different to showing or feeling compassion for others. You recognise that you are suffering, that you are having a hard time. You want to respond to the situation. Your heart aches with the pain, but you have a desire to do something to change the situation. You understand that this is part of life. Instead of ignoring the pain, you reflect on how you can ease the discomfort. You are kind to yourself. Kindness also leads to an increase in self-compassion.

What self-compassion isn't is self-pity. It doesn't mean you become immersed in your own problems and forget that other people may be hurting too. You still stay connected to those around you. It allows you to see what is happening in your own life and also relate it to other people.

Self-compassion is also different from being self-indulgent. You may feel you don't want to consider this, as it feels like you are putting yourself at the centre of everything. In one sense you are, but what you are doing is with good reason. You are not being selfish. It means that you will be happier and healthier in the long-term. It may also be considered a weak thing to do but that's not the case either. Jesus climbed up a mountain to have the space and time he needed.

Being kind to yourself

Alison Fox is a practising counsellor, psychotherapist and clinical supervisor based in Weymouth in Dorset. In recent years, working with people who are experiencing all kinds of mental health issues such as eating disorders, childhood abuse, depression, anxiety, stress and increasingly, people living with trauma, encouraging people to 'be kind' to themselves has become important. She spends a lot of time talking about kindness.

She told Cathy:

> If you're thinking about anxiety as an example, then often people will be experiencing intrusive thoughts and feelings of guilt and with that goes low mood. So, if people are kind to themselves in their thinking, and then in their behaviours towards themselves and allow themselves time to rest and give themselves permission to rest, the likelihood is that those intrusive thoughts will be less intensive.

Being kind to yourself can look different for everyone. It could be quite simple, like taking time for ourselves, having a cup of tea with a friend, taking some exercise.

But it can also mean changing the way we think and the way we talk to ourselves, challenging critical thoughts by thinking more positively. It may also be about setting clear boundaries, having a bit more balance in our lives, and perhaps even allowing ourselves permission not to do the things that don't nourish us. Maybe even 'rewarding' ourselves from time to time.

This can be tricky for all sorts of reasons. Maybe we don't want to be seen as self-centred or perhaps we don't have much experience of kindness in our own lives. Alison explains:

> If you haven't experienced kindness yourself then it's a completely alien concept, while for other people it's all about self-worth and thinking that other people deserve it more than they do. Either that's because they've been traumatised in some way or they've been conditioned to think that way.

Often, we may be really good at being kind to other people, but *we* get missed out in the process. Alison says:

> If you've got low self-worth then you're not going to think that you're worth it. Other people are 'worth it' so it's OK to be kind to them or for them to treat themselves, but to say, 'I'm allowed to speak kindly to myself and give myself things that nurture me' can be really challenging.

Alison is not just a counsellor, but also a Christian, and so she knows that the concept of being kind to ourselves can be fraught with confusion, especially if we've grown up learning that others must come first.

Earlier we learnt about the 'Golden Rule' which cuts across faith and time and which Jesus referred to in his Sermon on the Mount, documented for us in Matthew 7:12: 'Do to others what you would have them do to you.'

'I talk to people about this all the time,' Alison says. But she believes it can be open to misinterpretation and that most people may interpret it as putting others before themselves:

> It doesn't say, 'Don't do it to yourself as well.' For me, as a Christian, my relationship with God just isn't like that at all. So, maybe I'm completely wrong and I'm talking to a different God to everybody else, but my God says to me 'rest . . . I love you . . . I want the best for you . . .' I think it means treat others as well as yourself not instead of yourself.
>
> You give to others because you are coming from a place of rest and love. We're not to be a martyr . . . that's missing the point. Jesus was the martyr so that we don't have to be martyred.

So, even if putting yourself before others, it's worth considering being kind to yourself. Part of Alison's work is to help people become aware of the issues that challenge them and their mental wellbeing and, sometimes, helping them to find satisfaction with who they are, to stop criticising themselves and to stop trying to solve all the problems in the world.

To help others, she often uses the words of the Serenity Prayer,[5] written by the American theologian Reinhold Niebuhr (1892–1971), the first four lines of which might help us all from time to time:

> God, grant me the serenity to accept the things I cannot change; courage to change the things I can; and wisdom to know the difference.

Kindness is contagious

Kindness is something that can change us. It is also something that we can pass on to others and it can be contagious. Bridget LeRoy in an article in the *World Tribune* in 2016 wrote an article called, 'Is Kindness Contagious?'[6] In the article she discusses the fact that there have been a series of well-publicised studies published in the past decade proving that kindness is contagious. She highlights the fact that the behaviour of being kind or even watching someone being kind can spread from one person to others in a ripple effect of happiness. The original research was by James Fowler and Nicholas Christakis in the *British Medical Journal* who showed that emotion and behaviour can be transferred from one individual to another by mimicry or what they call 'emotional contagion'.[7]

We know that we tend to mimic behaviour, following group behaviour. Just look at what happens when one person starts protesting about something. That negativity can quickly spread. If we copy kindness, then we can see that there are immediate personal benefits, such as the physiological changes that we looked at in previous chapters.

Kindness and happiness can spread between people who are in direct contact with each other. It can also spread through larger communities. A good example of this is the way emotions can be changed on a large scale through social media such as Facebook. It is suggested that online social networks may even magnify the intensity of global emotional synchrony.

During the height of the first surge of the COVID-19 pandemic I joined a couple of Facebook groups to keep myself updated with what was happening in the world. One of them provided photos from people's windows. It was an extraordinary look into the lives of people across the world who were impacted by the pandemic. What no one could predict was that this group of strangers that shared glimpses of their lives were also kind to one another. Positive, affirming comments were left on people's posts. Some people really connected – offering help and support. People in need were contacted by others in the group. Practical help delivered via Amazon; gifts sent through the post. People connected. Kindness blossomed and people were happy being a part of this group. I loved it!

Practical pointers

These are some practical things we can do at an individual level that help kindness to grow. They are as follows:

1. Each morning when you get up think of at least one kind thing you can do.
2. Be self-aware. Consider what is going on around you. What are the needs of people in your community?
3. Seek out opportunities. Be thankful for even the little things.

4. Be kind to yourself.
5. Be kind to the people closest to you.
6. Keep a journal of this journey.

Summary

We know that giving or receiving kindness has a positive impact on the individual. We also know that kindness can have a positive impact on our self-esteem, our self-efficacy and self-confidence. What we think about ourselves changes when we are exposed to kindness. If we are kind and perform kind acts, then we feel happiness and our satisfaction in life increases. And it is also contagious. We can pass it on, we can pay it forward.

Prayer

Father,
We are so grateful that you love us.
We are astounded by your grace to us.
We know that you sent your only Son to die in our place.
What can we say?
Thank you, thank you, thank you.
Amen.

6

The Impact of Kindness on Society

Cathy Le Feuvre

A single act of kindness throws out roots in all directions, and the roots spring up and make new trees.

Amelia Earhart[1]

In recent years some friends of mine, the Revd Elaine and Revd Graeme Halls, moved after many years in the Channel Islands to a new home in Wales. Retirement beckoned for the pair after a lifetime spent in Christian ministry including, for Graeme, more than a decade as the Methodist Superintendent in Jersey. I followed their journey on social media and delighted in seeing how they settled into their new rural home and set up a smallholding, including some hens who soon got down to laying eggs.

Then COVID-19 hit and the couple, like many millions across the globe, faced lockdown and isolation. That's when they decided to stretch out the hand of kindness and friendship to their neighbours. As lockdown began, they wrote a note and delivered it to all the houses in their end of the hamlet that had become their home, offering to collect shopping and prescriptions and do similar simple kindnesses for others. The small village they live in is so remote that they don't even have door numbers, just names. So, to explain who it was that was writing, and who it was that was sending the note, they described where they lived as 'the house with the "eggs for sale" sign outside'.

'Within hours we had phone calls, not from people needing things, but appreciative of our kindness,' Elaine explains. But that was just the start of the development of new relationships.

> Then egg orders came in and soon egg customers were leaving empty boxes by their doors with money inside for the egg delivery man to exchange for a full box of eggs. After a while, egg customers became friends. It just shows what a bit of kindness can reap.

Kindness repaid by friendship and bringing neighbours and community together. Now that's a powerful thought. But the question is, can simply being kind really impact our society? And does kindness really 'spread', or is that just something that we humans would like to believe?

Johann Wolfgang von Goethe was a German polymath in the late eighteenth and early nineteenth century. He's considered to be the greatest German literary figure of modern times, but he wasn't just a poet, playwright, novelist, theatre director and critic, but also a statesman and scientist. In addition to his plays, poetry and literature, he also investigated and wrote about anatomy, botany and colour. Kindness also came under Johann's spotlight. He once described kindness as 'the golden chain by which society is bound'.[2] This concept of kindness being able to transform our societies is one that has received a lot of aesthetic, academic and scientific attention down the decades but in recent years, especially during the global COVID-19 pandemic, there's been more interest in how kindness motivates us and how it might alter the world in which we live.

There have been masses of human studies down the years, some of which determined to analyse what kindness is specifically, but others which dealt with human happiness. And kindness appears to be part of that.

Givers, Receivers and Controls

One widely cited piece of research into kindness and its impact, particularly in the workplace, was undertaken by researchers from the University of California involving mostly female workers at the Coca-Cola plant in Madrid in Spain.[3] The workforce thought they were taking part in research to measure levels of job satisfaction and happiness at work and to look at relationships with their colleagues, but what they didn't know was that they were randomly being divided into groups . . . Givers, Receivers and Controls.

All the staff received instructions for how they were expected to behave for the duration of the study. Over a period of four weeks the 'Givers' were asked to do five acts of kindness for a personalised list of colleagues (the 'Receivers'). Just small kindnesses like thanking them for their work, or getting them a drink.

Scientifically, these favours are what is known as prosocial behaviour,[4] which are actions intended to help others (we looked at the term 'prosocial' earlier in this book). The term 'prosocial' was framed in the 1970s when social scientists wanted a word to describe the opposite of 'antisocial' behaviours. Prosocial includes cooperating, helping, sharing, comforting and feeling empathy and concern for others as well as being concerned for the feelings and welfare and even rights of those around us.

There's a website called Prosocial World which is home to a non-profit organisation that 'seeks to evolve a more prosocial world'[5] and is inspired by science – they base their methods '. . . on the most recent developments in evolutionary, complex systems, and contextual behavioural science to enhance cooperation and inspire positive change for the wellbeing of others.'[6] This all sounds a bit enormous, doesn't it? But kindness is *that* important. Because even if we don't know it, those small acts of kindness are not just about our actions and attitudes, but it can be much bigger than that, as the Prosocial World website announces:

'The word "prosocial" describes an orientation toward the welfare of others and society as a whole. This might be an attitude, a behaviour, or an institution. It might be directed toward family and friends or the social acceptance of all people. Ultimately, Prosocial is an entire worldview.'[7] Kindness fits perfectly into that prosocial description. If we are 'orientated' towards kindness, it isn't just about us.

In the Coca-Cola research study, with 'Controls' also in place – workers who weren't assigned any tasks – the researchers had comparisons to judge against their findings, and the team, led by Professor Joseph Chancellor, set about observing the workforce and their responses. And the results, published in 2018, were astonishing.

In the short-term, within the four weeks of the study during which the Coca-Cola staff were monitored on a weekly basis, wellbeing, competency and a sense of 'autonomy' increased for both groups. But in the long-term, the benefits were there too. Those within the 'Receivers' group became happier after two months and 'Givers' identified being less depressed and more satisfied with their jobs and their lives in general.

Most importantly, the prosocial behaviours inspired other to act. 'Receivers' paid the acts of kindness forward with

278 per cent more prosocial behaviours than those who, unbeknown to them, had been placed in the 'Controls' group.[8]

The researchers concluded: 'Our results reveal that practicing everyday prosociality is both emotionally reinforcing and contagious (inspiring kindness and generating hedonic rewards in others) and that receiving everyday prosociality is an unequivocally positive experience . . .'[9]

Even after the study was concluded, the effects of a month of concentrated kindness in the workplace seemed to be still having an impact. Those who had been at the receiving end of the small acts of kindness were not only reporting being happier, but they said they had started to do more favours for others . . . around three times more than their 'Control' colleagues. And they weren't just doing kindnesses for the people they had received favours from (the 'Givers'), but for others outside that circle.

In other words, they were 'paying forward' the acts of kindness they had received.

Who goes first?

So, it appears that when someone does something kind for us, apart from making us feel happy and included and perhaps 'worthy' of such a kindness, it encourages us to act similarly. A simple example for us to consider is one we may all have experienced in our lives. We arrive at a venue and we and another person, perhaps someone we know or a complete stranger, find ourselves at the door, or the lift, at the same time.

Question – who goes first?

Will we prefer the other person over ourselves? Will we open the door for them, or at least indicate that we would like them to proceed ahead of us? Or do we actually not see the other person at all and just rush for the door and make sure we are out of that lift or that room or that building as soon as is physically possible?

When someone opens a door for us or allows us to enter a room before them, it makes us feel great, if only for a split second. (That is, unless we are a completely self-centred person who thinks, 'Yes, I deserve that, I *am* entitled to be first!') And, I don't know about you, but the knock-on effect is that we then want to return the favour.

Have you played the 'No, after *you*!' game? I have. We nod to the other person, they stand back a little, we tilt our head and smile: 'No . . . after *you*!' They maybe indicate that they want us to step forward first. The game can go on for quite a while, but sooner or later one steps forward, taking advantage of the other's kindness in letting them go first.

Then what often happens? Well, in my case, if someone for instance lets me in the lift before them, when we arrive at our floor, I make way for them to exit first. The first kindness has given way to a second. And who knows where that second prosocial act may lead? Maybe to a whole world of increased politeness, unselfishness and kindness? We can but hope!

Although these types of small kindnesses might not change the world, they may well change that moment in time for the person at the receiving end of that 'act of kindness'.

None of us know what others are experiencing or what life is like for them, unless they are very close to us and we know their story intimately. By being considerate – perhaps by opening that shop door so the mum with overflowing bags can get to her car more quickly, or perhaps saying 'thank you' to the busy bank clerk or the person spending hours ringing up the products on the supermarket till, or making a cup of tea for a colleague at work when we are making our own cuppa – we do not know the impact our actions may have. Just those small 'favours' which cost us nothing could be the bright spark in a person's day! This is kindness not for ourselves but for others. It's that kindness which comes naturally, just like breathing, and of which, as Christians, the Bible reminds us on many occasions.

What Paul teaches us

In the New Testament, Paul writes letters to the very young church in the Greek town of Philippi. If you know your Bible, you'll be aware that Paul, previously called 'Saul', was a religious Jewish leader determined to persecute the Christians in the years just after Jesus' time on earth. But following a miraculous 'conversion' on the road to a town called Damascus (in present-day Syria) he 'met' the spirit and person of Jesus and was converted. His life was turned around and his mission thereafter was to do all he could to share the gospel or good news of Jesus Christ.

Paul became an apostle, an ardent follower of Jesus and an itinerant missionary who spent many years travelling, spreading the 'Jesus Way' of love, kindness, compassion and justice to the expanding Christian churches, including into Europe. He visited Philippi several times and later, while he was imprisoned in Rome for sharing his faith, he wrote a series of letters including to his friends in Philippi, to encourage them in their faith.

These letters are in the New Testament as the book of Philippians and in chapter 2 verses 1–4 he gives advice about being humble in faith.

> Therefore if you have any encouragement from being united with Christ, if any comfort from his love, if any common sharing in the Spirit, if any tenderness and compassion, then make my joy

> complete by being like-minded, having the same love, being one in spirit and of one mind. Do nothing out of selfish ambition or vain conceit. Rather, in humility value others above yourselves, not looking to your own interests but each of you to the interests of the others.

Paul goes on to urge his friends in Philippi to have the same mindset as Jesus, who lived a life where serving others was paramount – the 'Jesus Kindness' way of life we read about earlier.

'No . . . after *you*!' Not *me* first . . . but others! Valuing others and their needs above our own. A contagious type of kindness which may change the world.

Humans are hardwired for kindness

In his book *Humankind: A Hopeful History*,[10] the internationally bestselling author and historian Rutger Bregman sets out to argue against the belief that human beings are born selfish and there's not much we can do about it.

Bregman believes it's time to look again at human nature and at the history of humankind. As he explores 200,000 years of human history, and looks again at some of the major events, literature and research that seems to have reinforced the notion that humans are bad, Bregman seeks to prove that humans are 'hardwired' for kindness, and that we are more likely to cooperate than not, and that trust comes naturally rather than distrust of others.

Forget all we've been told, including from philosophers ancient and modern, psychologists, writers and even today's news media, which would have us believe those headlines that indicate that the world is in a constant crisis where people are invariably inclined to murder, loot and pillage and think only of themselves. Bregman's book is stuffed full of examples of where that is simply not the case.

Bregman admits that this is a 'radical idea' that even religious leaders might feel uncomfortable embracing, but he believes if we take this seriously, it might 'turn society on its head'.[11] As the title of his first chapter indicates, it's 'A New Realism'.

His Epilogue, which he comes to after a host of engaging storytelling which delves back in time and debunks many 'myths' which would have us believe that people are essentially self-centred if not entirely 'bad', is a list of 'Ten Rules to Live By' if we want to live with the more positive view of humanity.

Bregman's ninth 'rule' is this . . . 'Come out of the closet: don't be ashamed to do good'.[12]

Although he doesn't appear to be writing from a particularly spiritual perspective, Bregman reminds us that Jesus warned on the Sermon on the Mount not to brag when we give to the needy, but that he also encourages us to let people see the good things we do.

You are a light to the world

In Matthew we read Jesus' instructions:

> You are the light of the world. A town built on a hill cannot be hidden. Neither do people light a lamp and put it under a bowl. Instead they put it on its stand, and it gives light to everyone in the house. In the same way, let your light shine before others, that they may see your good deeds and glorify your Father in heaven.
>
> *Matthew 5:14–16*

The delicate balance between showing kindness and those 'prosocial behaviours' without drawing too much attention to and taking the glory for ourselves can be tricky, which Bregman admits: 'To extend that hand you need one thing above all. Courage.' Even if you're 'branded a bleeding heart or a show-off' by doing those kind things.[13] But his conclusion is inspiring: 'Every good deed is like a pebble in a pond, sending ripples out in all directions . . . Kindness is catching and it's so contagious that it even infects people who merely see it from afar', he writes, citing a case explored by the psychologist Jonathan Haidt, who studied the effect of this type of 'infectious' morality.[14]

Bregman explains:

> Haidt discovered that people are often surprised and moved by simple acts of generosity. When the psychologist asked his research subjects how this kind of experience affected them, they described an irresistible urge to go out and help others. Haidt calls this emotion 'elevation'. People are wired so that a simple act of kindness literally makes us feel warm and tingly. And what's fascinating is that this effect occurs even when we hear these stories from someone else. It's as though we press a mental reset button that wipes away our cynical feelings, so we once more have a clear view of the world.[15]

The idea of kindness as a way of 'elevating' human culture and behaviour is so intriguing, and challenging. As you're reading this book, then I'm guessing you may be interested in the general concept of kindness and its impact, and may already be asking yourself questions like:

- How can I make kindness a central feature of my nature? Something that does just come naturally to me, like breathing?

- Is it too late for me to 'learn' to be kind?
- If I do reach out to others, will I do it to expect something back or just be confident in the knowledge that I've helped someone, and maybe that might rub off on them and perhaps they might do something similar down the line for someone else?

No agendas, no expectations – whether they are thought-out kindnesses, planned in advance and directed at a particular person or group or circumstance which you are aware of, kindness deliberately offered to another, or just acts of random kindness which are the response to situations which crop up and 'just happen' and are over as quickly as they arise.

Are we secure enough in ourselves and gracious enough towards others to just know that we are part of that kindness 'golden chain' by which society is bound, that we heard about earlier from the German politician and writer Johann Wolfgang von Goethe?

Kindness can be socially transformative, there's no doubt about that. But that sounds very large scale, so maybe it's easier for us to start small and work from there. To start just living those small kindnesses which make an impact on those around us.

One final story, I hope, will inspire us to this 'kindness living'.

I spoke to Marilyn Carré when I was helping a small local charity with its 'pop-up' art installation and shop during a week of awareness raising around domestic abuse, where the emphasis was on the impact of 'coercive behaviour'.

But the first time I met Marilyn was back in the 1990s when she had set up and was running Jersey's first rape crisis counselling service. Down the years, she has used her training as a social worker and as a psychotherapist to benefit the island community and people who are hurt and in crisis. She was one of the pioneers who helped set up the Jersey Women's Refuge, has worked as a child care officer, a probation officer and in many more 'caring' roles.

So, you could say that Marilyn is the epitome of kindness; she's spent her life helping others, caring and sharing her skills and her compassion. She's woven it into her professional life, but at this latest meeting I discovered that kindness seems to be embedded in her DNA.

At the time we met and chatted, Marilyn was having some major work done at home – the windows and doors were being replaced. A messy old business which obviously involves workmen traipsing through the property and being there at all hours of the day.

Now, some of us might just want it all to be over, to leave the house while the work is being done every day, not to have to look at the mess or feel the breeze through the open gaps in the walls; to just leave the workmen to it.

Not Marilyn. Instead, she was determined that the whole experience would be one that everyone would enjoy.

Every day during the project she invited the workers to take a break, sit down at her table and join her for lunch.

And why does she do this simple kindness? Marilyn told me when I pressed her for information:

> Because they're really sweet, they're lovely. There's a young apprentice who doesn't stop smiling and is just so gorgeous and then I have the other people, they come at different times. And the weather's been on and off, a bit chilly and miserable and they work so hard, and they start at . . . anytime between seven and half-past seven in the morning . . . so I make sure that they have a choice of soups and crusty bread for lunch. And tea and coffee throughout the day.

And then she went on to explain that the reason she did this small kindness every day, was because of her own dad's experiences, but in a different way:

> I do it because my father was a stonemason and years ago, he told me that very often he would go all day and nobody would give him even a cup of tea or a glass of water and if they did, it was out of a chipped mug. So, I make sure that they sit down with me, we sit down together and we have the same cups and the same plates and the same saucers . . . and we just have lunch together.

And there's more. Her kindness had become a circle during the project. She also offered lunch because those young skilled workmen were kind to her.

> They've been so lovely, and they've gone out of their way to make sure that everything is beautifully tidied at the end of the day. If I say, 'Look, you leave that – I can vacuum later' they reply, 'No, we want to leave it nicely for you!'

It's a small thing, born out of not just Marilyn's own sense of kindness, the kindness she has received but also because of her own father's experience of *not* being treated kindly. Negative experiences can lead to bitterness and anger. But for Marilyn, it's the impetus to be as kind as possible, at every opportunity.

As she reminded me: 'If the love goes around, everybody's happy!'

Practical pointers

Try to do one simple act of kindness each day.

That may be just offering someone a cup of tea or letting someone go before you in the queue at the supermarket till. Do they only have a few items to buy in comparison to your loaded trolley? Will you make them wait for you to finish, or allow them to go first and be out of that shop in a jiffy?

Let's be intentional in our kindness.

Summary

We're learning that kindness can be 'infectious', that one act of kindness can lead to another. And when we start to think of the kindnesses we do as part of that 'golden chain by which society is bound' which Johann Wolfgang von Goethe imagined, we may begin to see that we could actually be part of a movement to change the world. However, for most of us that worldview might seem rather overwhelming and unattainable, so perhaps we may just start with our own (albeit small) circle of influence. The Coca-Cola workers in Madrid who were assigned roles as 'Givers' in the kindness study would not have known that their part in the experiment would rub off on others, but it did! And they didn't do anything spectacular, just small 'prosocial' kindnesses, acts which quickly made a difference to the lives of their co-workers and made *them* want to act similarly.

But here's the challenge for us and a question we need to ask ourselves – are we, as the website Prosocial World advises, 'orientated' towards the welfare of others and society as a whole?[16] In other words, is our natural inclination towards being kind or do we need to reset our kindness compass? Do we *look* for opportunities to be kind? Are our minds and hearts wired to seek out kindnesses, or is it a bit of an effort? Are we conscious that our attitudes and actions can adversely or positively affect their lives and actions in response to how we have treated them?

If we think we might need a change of perspective . . . perhaps we might like to pray about it.

Prayer

Lord,
Thank you for the privilege of being part of your world, and the community you have placed me in.
Open my eyes to the opportunities for kindness. Soften my heart and make me sensitive to the needs of others, even those people who I might not be naturally drawn to. I'm sorry for the times when I have deliberately decided against stepping out of my comfort zone to extend the hand of kindness. Just as you put others first, help me to value others and their needs. Every day, give me moments when I might be able to show small kindnesses without a thought of what I might gain from it.
May I become part of that golden chain of kindness, and may the small kindnesses you lead me to be the start of ripples in a pond that inspires others.
Amen.

7

The Rise of Kindness During the Pandemic

Cathy Le Feuvre

No act of kindness, no matter how small, is ever wasted.

Aesop[1]

In early March 2020 the World Health Organization declared a global COVID-19 pandemic. We were glued to our television screens, radios and technical devices as we witnessed the illness spreading like wildfire across the globe. The daily death toll started escalating and across the world, healthcare systems, including the National Health Service in the UK, were becoming overwhelmed.

We entered the year 2020 with so much optimism in the air but within a few short weeks we found ourselves at the start of this terrifyingly unknown pandemic. COVID-19, coronavirus – we couldn't escape it. Scientists worked frantically to find a vaccine which, thankfully, came within a year, but for most of us there was no option. If we were to avoid infection and death, we needed to 'isolate'. No face-to-face engagements. Governments 'locked down' their communities. One hour exercise a day out and about. No visits with family and friends. No mass gatherings. No church.

We quickly learned a new vocabulary – social distancing, physical distancing, hand-sanitising, mask-wearing, Zoom and other online calling. Lockdown.

On 18 May 2020, at the height of the first COVID-19 'lockdown' in Jersey in the Channel Islands, an ice cream van parked up in the main carpark at the General Hospital in the island's principal town of St Helier.

Over the next few hours Stuart Young, local ice cream vendor extraordinaire, handed out 760 free ice creams to those working tirelessly in the hospital to save lives, from the doctors and consultants to the nurses and carers, those in administration and the army of people doing so-called 'menial tasks' without which a hospital just doesn't operate. There was no 'first in line' or preferential treatment. Everyone who came got a treat, everyone got a smile from Stuart, and there's no doubt that everyone came away with their hearts lifted and a sense of belonging to a community that *cared* for those who were caring for us.

A wonderful story, I'm sure you'll agree, but what made this act of kindness and generosity even more spectacular is that Stuart decided to hand out the tasty treats . . . on his own birthday!

Stuart didn't do this for publicity, although when local media found out about it, they of course wanted to share the story, and it did make local television and radio bulletins as well as being covered in the local newspapers – physical and online. It was just one of many examples of kindness which we saw during the pandemic and those lockdowns which kept us indoors, isolated, physically distanced, sanitised up to the elbows and apart from our loved ones.

For Stuart, it wasn't a spontaneous act of kindness. Because of all the COVID-19 restrictions and health regulations which so defined the pandemic lockdowns, it took four weeks to set up, to gain all the necessary permissions to make it happen.

But for Stuart it was a way not just of thanking the medical community for the many hours, days, weeks and months that had already been spent caring for the island's population and keeping residents alive in a global pandemic. It was also a way of saying 'thanks' for something that happened many years ago when one of the hospital consultants brought hope back into his family. Stuart says:

> He saved my daughter's life, and he did so much for my twins, who are now healthy. He did save them. And I also did it because I went through cancer, and I wanted to give something back.

Stuart has been selling ice creams at Gorey on Jersey's east coast for forty years, so he's well-known in the community. And it's not the first time he's shown such kindness. He gives out ice creams to those working through the night in the parish of Grouville to build extravagant floral floats which are often award-winners in Jersey's annual floral parade – the Battle of Flowers. He's been involved for many years in Variety, the children's charity, which supports families and young people in need across the island. He's got involved in charity fundraising events galore and on 9 May he hands out ice creams to older people to celebrate the Liberation Day annual festivities, which mark the day in 1945 that the Channel Islands were 'liberated' after nearly five years of German occupation during the Second World War.

Speak to Stuart's staff, and they'll tell you quite simply that he is a very kind man, and Stuart himself believes that kindness is not just personal but community: 'Kindness comes from the heart really and here in Jersey we're a tight community and it makes me proud to help. I was brought up that way. My mum used to say, "Stuart, always look after the next one, always think of someone else", and I've always done that and tried to keep it. I'm a great believer in "what goes around comes around"', he explained as he leaned out of his ice-cream van and handed a very small free ice cream cone to a customer's dog, something he also does quite regularly.

People like Stuart have always been around, thank God. People who just live kindness, people who feel that it is part of their humanity to live out kindness, to support and care for individuals, even those they do not know personally. It's a value he grew up learning from his family, his mum, and something he feels is a duty to perpetuate, as well as a joy.

The COVID-19 global pandemic which has so badly impacted our world since the outbreak of the coronavirus in early 2020 was, and still is, devastating: heart-breaking for families and those who have lost loved ones, devastating for some parts of the economy, traumatic for those who lost their jobs, and overwhelming and stressful for many who kept our services open, including those health professionals working day in, day out wrapped up in Personal Protective Equipment (PPE) to try to save lives – sometimes unsuccessfully.

But one upside, if there is such a thing of the pandemic, is people like Stuart and millions more who, when the world needed it, turned to kindness. Although some of the kindness 'acts' and 'events', like the ice cream extravaganza at Jersey General Hospital, were planned; many more were spontaneous and some of the perpetrators may not have even realised that what they were doing epitomised 'kindness'.

As we write this book, the pandemic is still in progress, although now we are learning to live with it, and in many parts of the world vaccines are helping to reduce mortality. We know there is still the threat of further lockdowns and 'circuit breakers' when or if the rates of infection and deaths rise, and some people are suffering the long-term effects of contracting the virus with what is generically known as 'Long Covid'. But it feels like some sort of normality is returning with some gatherings. And at least most of us, here in Jersey and the UK anyway, can sing out loud again. In church! How we missed that. There's something about singing that lifts the spirit, isn't there?

Something that filled me with joy at the height of the pandemic and which is one of the overwhelming memories that will stay in my mind long after, God willing, our world has a handle on COVID-19, is rainbows!

Rainbows in windows, stuck with sticky tape from the inside so that people could see them when passing the house. Rainbows drawn expertly as part of art installations and those drawn in crayons by little ones. Rainbows sometimes accompanied by a simple phrase like 'We care' or 'Take care' or 'Be safe'.

Rainbows in collage, covered in multicoloured paper flowers. Rainbows drawn on pebbles and rocks which cropped up in random places, left there by people, including many children, who had no idea who might find them or when.

Rainbows and rainbow makers came in all shapes and sizes, and it was a way of sharing kindness and hope at a time when we were desperate for both.

The rainbow is an ancient sign of hope, but as I noticed all those lovely images popping up all over the place, including virtually and online, I often wondered if the makers and creators realised that they were part of many centuries of hope and part of a spiritual tradition, even if they were unaware of it.

Whenever I saw those rainbows, I was reminded of the story of Noah, about whom we read in the first book of the Bible. He is the man, of course, who listened to God and built an ark for his family and for animals galore, which were then saved from a devastating flood. His hard work and faith in the uncertain times he was living through, is inspiring. And once the flood waters went down and Noah and his family were back on dry land, God made a 'covenant' with him, a promise . . . and he showed him a rainbow in the sky which would be the constant sign of that agreement and God's kindness and goodness. It's all there in Genesis.

> 'This is the sign of the covenant I am making between me and you and every living creature with you, a covenant for all generations to come. I have set my rainbow in the clouds, and it will be the sign of the covenant between me and the earth. Whenever I bring clouds over the earth and the rainbow appears in the clouds, I will remember my covenant between me and you and all living creatures of every kind. Never again will the waters become a flood to destroy all life. Whenever the rainbow appears in the clouds, I will see it and remember the everlasting covenant between God and all living creatures of every kind on the earth.' So God said to Noah, 'This is the sign of the covenant I have established between me and all life on the earth.'
>
> *Genesis 9:12–17*

Sometimes the COVID-19 pandemic felt like a bit of a flood, I'm sure you'll agree. It came in waves and seemed to be overwhelming, but those rainbows in windows and on the side of the road and all over social media constantly reminded me that we were, we are, not alone.

And suddenly, kindness became a buzzword. People 'rediscovered' a value which has always been there, but which is sometimes buried under negativity and cynicism. Although, as we've read earlier, some of us believe that kindness comes naturally to humans, sometimes it gets lost in our world where we may think more about ourselves than others.

The COVID-19 pandemic is not the first time that crisis has resulted in kindness. Earlier I mentioned that during the Second World War, the Channel Islands were held under Nazi occupation for nearly five years, from July 1940 to May 1945. And across those years there were tremendous acts of kindness. People shared their increasingly meagre rations, and were hiding Jewish friends from the authorities to prevent them from being arrested and taken away, sometimes putting themselves in peril. Such selfless acts of kindness and compassion have been and still are existent across the world; it seems times of conflict and catastrophe can bring out the best in humans.

But for many, the pandemic experience will have been the first time they have really stopped to reflect on kindness.

The word was everywhere.

In Australia, clinicians set up the Pandemic Kindness Movement to support all health workers during the COVID-19 crisis. They '. . . curated respected, evidence-informed resources and links to valuable services to support the wellbeing of the health workforce'[2] and made it easily accessible.

The team behind the Pandemic Kindness Movement used a model called the 'Pyramid of Needs' based on the world-renowned 'Hierarchy of Needs' motivational theory in psychology created by the twentieth-century American psychologist, Abraham Maslow.

His five-tier pyramid of needs are, from the bottom up, physiological (food and clothing), safety (job security), love and belonging needs (friendship), esteem, and self-actualisation. The needs at the lower end of the pyramid must be satisfied before people can progress to the next level.[3]

Notice that love and belonging needs or friendship lie right at the heart of Maslow's Hierarchy of Needs. That includes kindness, without which humans might not 'progress' to the next level. The pyramid representing the needs of the Australian health workforce also has kindness at its centre. At ground level there were basic needs, then safety, love and belonging, esteem, contribution and in this case, leadership actions were placed at the top.

At every level, those Australian health professionals and caregivers could access resources to help them whatever stage they felt they were at, and in the 'Loving and Belonging' section in the centre of the pyramid there was the subtext of 'kindness, community and social connection' which was explained like this:

> In this level of the pyramid, our needs are met through relationships with others that are based on inclusion and acceptance. COVID-19 is challenging our relationships across our society. We keep our distance physically, which means keeping connected emotionally is more important than ever.[4]

Encouraging people to be kind became important, especially in the early months of the pandemic when most of us were unable to leave our homes other than for essential shopping or healthcare.

At the BBC across the United Kingdom and the British Isles, producers, reporters and presenters at BBC Local Radio were tasked with encouraging people to share what they were doing to 'Make a Difference' in their community.[5] Eventually it resulted in 'campaigns'. One of the first was a call out to donate a laptop to help a child being home-schooled – but initially it was all about the little stories of kindnesses that people were grateful for.

Although the media played and still plays an important role in 'promoting' human kindness at times like a global pandemic, some more cynical observers might think that they're just jumping on a bandwagon. But for those of us who've worked for many years in the media, being able to report on good news rather than the endless diet of bad news was and is refreshing. To be able to balance words like 'crisis' and 'disaster' with words like 'love', 'compassion', 'friendship' and 'kindness' is a joy!

Yes, lots of people did jump on the kindness train, albeit only for a while. How many websites did you see with titles like 'Ten kind things you can do during the COVID-19 pandemic'? Comment and advice came from all sources, even perhaps unlikely ones like *Glamour* magazine in the UK, which ran a headline that said: 'How to *actually* be kind during the Coronavirus pandemic' and a subheading which implored us all to 'ensure this sense of community long outlasts the pandemic'.[6]

There's no doubt we could quote many media, 'government' and other large-scale kindly programmes and services which were birthed during the pandemic, but perhaps more important were the 'small scale' and individual responses to the needs of others, as these came about because people really cared. They cared about what was happening to others.

In the past, acts of kindness were often physical – in person. People offering to go shopping for their neighbours, popping in for a cuppa to ensure an elderly neighbour wasn't becoming isolated, smiling at the stranger in the street. That, of course, must still endure, but during lockdowns all that goodwill could have dried up.

Shaking hands as a greeting was out . . . no touching. So don't think about hugs! Smiling at someone in the street was a challenge when we were all wearing masks. Who could see that smile? And that was if we could get out during lockdowns when our movements were so restricted.

So, people had to find new ways to connect, and across the world, social media was the obvious choice.

Just one example . . . in Jersey when the first lockdown began on 30 March 2020, almost immediately a community Facebook page became a lifeline for many people. It was called 'Coronavirus Jersey – Acts of Kindness' and the concept was simple: to encourage islanders to share what they might have with others, especially those who couldn't get out, and even to offer advice on shops with essential items in stock. Besides the practical help, it was also designed as a place for friendship and moral support, and very quickly it became just that and continues to be an important community space.

'Coronavirus Jersey – Acts of Kindness' might have started life in lockdown, but it has a life beyond – at the time of writing, membership stands at nearly 10,000 members, with new people coming on board every week. The name has changed slightly – it's now called 'Jersey – Acts of Kindness' and these days it's a page where encouraging comments and ideas are shared along with charity fundraising and community information. But back in the early days, it was a forum for sharing information and resources, advice and appreciation, thanks and gratitude. At a time when we were getting used to using hand sanitiser and wearing masks, there were stories that reminded us to stay safe. People shared what they were doing to make masks and extra scrubs for hospital workers working under difficult circumstances on the wards. There was news of those colourfully painted rainbows and pebbles and the things people were doing to raise the spirits of others.

Down the months, the Facebook page became a real community – social media engagement at its very best. There was news of kindnesses offered in thanks to the many health professionals who were working tirelessly to get us through the pandemic, including drop-offs of fruit and other treats to Jersey's ICU.

Some of the messages were more personal, with thanks for individual kindnesses received, including flowers from a friend. Some members of the page took the opportunity to appeal for items which would make lockdown easier for others, such as books for an elderly person who was a voracious reader.

And among the many 'thank yous', appeals and postings were fun things like the sharing of recipes and the offer of scrumptious morsels to be enjoyed especially by those isolated at home.

The idea behind the Facebook page was brilliant in its simplicity:

- Some of us have more; let's share what we have with those who have less.
- Think about others as well as yourself.
- Some people have loads of support, many have no one – let's be that 'someone'.

That idea of standing together and being stronger together is compelling and it was a defining factor at the height of the pandemic.

Remember the 'Clap for Carers' every Thursday evening at 8 p.m.? The Facebook and social media communities were among those who encouraged us all to get out there and applaud those looking out for us during those early days of the pandemic.

At the end of December 2020, the Bailiff of Jersey handed out awards and citations to people who had given exemplary service to the community during the pandemic. These people were nominated by their fellow islanders and in total, forty-five islanders were recognised with a Bailiff's Award or a Bailiff's Citation[7] representing individuals from different sectors – health and emergency workers, people involved in the coronavirus helpline and the Government of Jersey's contact tracing service, and others caring for those affected by the pandemic during their working lives, or through charities, or just because they wanted to reach out to others. Among those were people making music online, looking after the elderly and families who were struggling to put food on the table because they had lost their jobs or were on furlough from their work and living in reduced circumstances.

The leaders of The Salvation Army church and charity organisation in Jersey, Alice and Richard Nunn, were among those honoured with a Bailiff's Award for their leadership and running of the Jersey Island Foodbank which every week put together and delivered hundreds of food and care parcels. However, as they told me, the award was not theirs but was really for the many kind and willing volunteers who stepped up to the challenge and came on board to help what was, at times, a military operation.

The Jersey Island Foodbank was a real celebration of kindness on a community level!

In Northern Ireland, where Debbie lives, there were multiple initiatives started just like in Jersey, supporting local communities. People made scrubs for hospital staff, baked cakes each week for weary staff and provided laptops and tablets for children stuck at home fighting over these devices to attend online classes. Debbie started 'Bags of Blessing' which is supported by her church, Dundonald Elim Church, and her local community. To date they have delivered more than 1,500 bags of toiletries to people stuck in hospital with COVID-19.

And this was happening all over the world – if you need convincing, just type the words 'pandemic acts of kindness' into an internet search engine and be prepared to be inundated with stories from around the globe.

There was the British teenager who was reported as having performed an act of kindness every day since the start of the pandemic.[8] A trio of students in Singapore collected food for distribution to low-income members of the community.[9] A landlord in the USA waived a month's rent to help his tenants who were worried about making ends meet.[10]

Just some of the many stories that may inspire at the click of a mouse. But all this is not new – it's something that we are encouraged to do in the Bible. In the Old Testament, we can read about the 'kindliness' of God and how that is passed down to his creation. And we learn how it is our job to 'pass it on'.

In the New Testament, there are different references and commands from Jesus himself for us to 'love one another' (John 13:34). We are taught in Galatians 5:22–23 that the 'fruit of the Spirit' includes 'love, joy, peace, patience, kindness, goodness, faithfulness, gentleness and self-control'. And in a letter received by the Colossians – a community of people in a place called Colossae in Asia Minor, in modern-day Turkey – early converts to Christianity in the years following the death and resurrection of Jesus Christ were encouraged to live a life of kindness and so much more.

> So, as those who have been chosen of God, holy and beloved, put on a heart of compassion, kindness, humility, gentleness and patience.
>
> *Colossians 3:12*, NASB

Although, as we've said before, values like kindness are not the sole domain of Christians, for followers of Jesus – those chosen by God – it is an imperative. Notice the Colossians aren't encouraged to 'think about' being kind, gentle, patient, humble and compassionate. They are directed to 'put on' those values.

Other translations, such as the NIV, tell the readers to 'clothe' themselves with those values.

As it's unlikely that we would go out without putting on some clothes (well, not unless we are really brave or stupid) so we are encouraged to put on the mantle of kindness and love . . . to be a walking example of compassion, humility, gentleness and patience – and kindness.

And this is not just for a one-off event. The challenge is now, for us all, to ensure that kind of kindness and love isn't just for a crisis. As God promised all those centuries ago to one faithful man, Noah, he's not just here for one or two people but for the whole of humankind! Forever.

But it's not a one-sided affair. I believe that we have a part to play in his plans for the wellbeing and future of humanity. Because while God gives us his unconditional love and promise, when we learn to be compassionate, hospitable, gentle, loving and kind, we somehow become part of God's plan to fill his world with love and kindness.

Of course, creating a kind world will be a long task, but one which will bring us all benefits. However, it may not all be an easy ride. Remember the ridicule that Noah received from his neighbours? Living that sort of value-laden life may well mean sacrifices – not just personal but financial.

If we need an example of that kind of life, we can of course look to Jesus. But also, to the many Stuarts of this world who have proved that living a life of kindness is worth the effort and commitment.

As he told me that afternoon, chatting to me from his ice cream van:

> It costs me, but I love it and it makes me proud to do it . . . it makes me feel good in my heart . . .

Practical pointers

We may not all have the resources to fund a big project or run a business where we can supply people with what they need. But we can pray – we know that changes things.

We can also give people time – time to listen or help. We can be creative and offer up ideas, helping others to catch a vision. We can simply offer a smile that is catching, and they too can pass it on.

What are you good at? If you are good at baking – drop off a cake to a neighbour who might be having a hard time. If you have time, offer to babysit for the stressed-out young mum who needs a break. Offer to cut the grass of the man down the street. Kindness looks like something and most of the time you recognise it straightaway.

And most importantly, be determined that you will keep doing all this long after the pandemic has passed.

Summary

There's no doubt that the world has been badly affected by the COVID-19 pandemic. Although at the time of writing we see glimpses of hope on the horizon, as different variants of the virus emerge, we are increasingly aware that we will probably have to live with it for a long while yet and may have to adapt to a different 'normal', as the world moves from a state of pandemic to a place where coronavirus is endemic and ever-present in our communities. But I believe that one of the true lights in the darkness was the kindness that we saw emerging organically, especially in the first swathe of lockdowns and restrictions in 2020.

The troubles we were all experiencing in some form or another seemed to bring the best out of many people, and even if they didn't know it, they were part of a sharing of God's love with the world. Of course, that's not to say that everyone became a kinder person – for some this era has sadly resulted in anger and even selfish behaviour. Not everyone reached out to others even when they saw them struggling, physically and emotionally, and unfortunately that has left many feeling even more isolated, rejected and sad than they would have been.

So let's think about the kindnesses we saw in our communities and ask ourselves . . . did *we* do enough for others? If we were able to go the extra mile to be kind to other people, did we do that? Or could we have done more? Could we do more in future? Might we need to just open our eyes and hearts a bit wider, especially to see those for whom the pandemic is having long-lasting repercussions?

Because the challenge now, as we go back to normal, or something resembling normal, is not to lose the kindness spirit which so engulfed so many of us and made us all the more generous and loving during times of crisis.

In person, and online, let's remember that kindness can be quite simple.

Prayer

Lord,

We pray for the world following this time of global pandemic. We pray for all those affected by illness, death, isolation, employment challenges and sadness. Help us to be the kindness which our community needs, not just in difficult times but every day, and to share your love and compassion with those we love, those we know and even those who we may not agree with.

Heavenly Father, as you promised us your enduring love, help us to love others and to be the kindness glue in our communities that binds us together.

In your precious name we pray.

Amen.

8

Do We Have Innate Kindness?

Debbie Duncan

That best portion of a good man's life, his little, nameless, unremembered, acts of kindness and love.

William Wordsworth[1]

I recently asked people on social media, 'What is the kindest thing anyone has ever done for you?' I was also interested to know who showed them such great kindness.

Jackie said it was when a friend sent her medical supplies and a letter of support when she was living in Africa. The fact that the person had put such thought and care and effort into it, made her feel looked after when she was vulnerable.

Claire told me it was 'the midwives that delivered her children safely into the world'.

Julia said it was her church group who sent meals after her son was born, meaning she didn't have to think about it when she was so exhausted.

Donna and her husband had to restart life in Belfast with their son who had a learning disability and a lady they did not know rented her house to them at a significantly reduced rent. Esther had her flights paid when she needed to raise the money to go to Gambia. Paul was given a car to use when his own car broke down.

Many were acts of kindness from friends or church members. There were, however, acts of great kindness from strangers. Sarah was given food when she needed it. Julia's husband was helped by several strangers when he was in a cycling accident. I have certainly been on the receiving end of this sort of kindness, and during the COVID-19 pandemic there have been great examples of acts of kindness from strangers. We read a bit about this in the previous chapter, and I am sure you can all think of examples too.

This did, however, make me wonder whether we are all born with the ability to be kind, particularly to people we don't know? After all, it is easier to be kind to friends and family. It's harder to be kind to a stranger.

Are we born kind?

We know that there are many psychologists who believe that we are born kind. There are many studies that suggest that our capacity for empathic awareness and altruism are built in.[2] They suggest that we are born with a kind mind, that we have some level of innate kindness.

The retired surgeon Ian Fraser considered kindness in the medical profession and suggests that kindness is an innate ability.[3] An innate ability is when a characteristic or ability is already present in a person when they are born. It is part of the ongoing debate about 'nature versus nurture' which is one of the oldest philosophical issues within psychology. Nature refers to all of the hereditary factors that influence who we are. This ranges from our physical appearance, such as the colour of our eyes, to our personality characteristics. Nurture, on the other hand, refers to all the environmental variables that impact who we are. This includes our early childhood development, our social relationships and the culture of the community we are a part of. This debate first came into use in the sixteenth century.

Dr David Hamilton, one of today's leading experts in the field of the mind–body connection, suggests that we are born kind, that each of us are born with kindness genes. One of the most important genes is the gene that helps produce the hormone oxytocin which is associated with reproduction, breastfeeding and social behaviour. As we read earlier, it is also called the 'love hormone' as oxytocin makes us love more and even makes us more kind. David Hamilton suggests that our kind nature is part of our core being.[4] Certainly, neuroscientists suggest that our brains are hard-wired for compassion, to be sympathetic and feel pity for the suffering of others. They suggest that we are born with the capacity for kindness.

In an aim to look at whether we are born kind or not, Paul Bloom researched this idea at the Infant Cognition Centre at Yale University in collaboration with Karen Wynn and Kiley Hamlin. Their work explores the moral life of babies. In the study, the researchers used puppets and showed that the majority of babies showed a strong preference for the puppet that was helpful over the one that wasn't.[5] The suggestion is that nature has a strong role in exhibiting kindness. Bloom does go on to suggest that humans have a rudimentary moral sense from birth.[6] This implies that it can be developed under the right circumstances.

The behavioural scientist Evan Nesterak states that the discussions about nature or nurture '. . . have more often led to ideological cul-de-sacs rather than pinnacles of insight'.[7] He suggests that the argument is more complicated than first thought with the development of epigenetics. This is the study of how any outside stimulus can cause genetic modifications. Epigenetics is the study of how cells control gene activity without changing the DNA sequence. It is called epigenetic because 'epi' means 'on' or 'above' in Greek. The epigenetic changes are modifications to DNA that regulate whether genes are turned on or off and can be transient or long-term. A common type of epigenetic modification is DNA methylation where methylation involves the attachment of small methyl groups to the DNA building blocks. When these methyl groups are attached onto a gene it turns the gene off, so it doesn't work properly. Another example is the chemical bisphenol A, found in many plastic compounds.

Psychologists believe that it is not just chemicals that cause these changes. They also believe that experiences can too. Epigenetic research demonstrates how genes and environments continuously interact to produce characteristics that can be passed through future generations. An example of this is that people who have gone through periods of starvation can pass on the impact of this to future generations. Childhood trauma can also impact our genes, which can be inherited in future generations. Adverse childhood experiences (ACEs) can cause epigenetic modifications leading to ACE-induced differential health outcomes such as cardiovascular disease, diabetes or bipolar disease.

Survivors of ACEs often have a set of negative core self-beliefs but there is evidence that religious beliefs can improve the response to psychotherapy for anxiety and depression.[8 9]

As Christians we know that God can change the story of our lives. Understanding what God says about us can change the words that are at the core of our life; the words that we believe about ourselves.

- You are 'fearfully and wonderfully made' (Ps. 139:14)
- You are precious to God (Ps. 139:16)

- You are loved (John 3:16)
- You are unique (Isa. 64:8)
- You are made in God's image (Gen. 1:27)
- You are God's child (Gal. 3:26)
- You are chosen (1 Pet. 2:9)
- You are God's workmanship (NASB) or 'masterpiece' (NLT) or 'handiwork' (NIV) (Eph. 2:10)
- You are valued (Matt. 10:29–31)

The question is – if our core qualities are not impacted by genetics or epigenetics, can we nurture and cultivate them? In Linda Kaplan Thaler and Robin Koval's book, *The Power of Nice: How to Conquer the Business World with Kindness* published in 2006,[10] the central idea is that some people are just born nice. The authors believe that they are just kind. They do more than five nice things a week that yield no personal gain.

Psychologists tells us that kindness can be nurtured and grown through practise, like using a muscle. The philosophers Giambattista Vico (1668–1744) and Anthony Cooper (the third Earl of Shaftesbury, 1671–1713) both recognised kindness as a moral emotion that is grown and cultivated in our social nature and is fundamental for society. They were Stoic philosophers who believed that there are three fundamental ideas (these are known as the Stoic Triangle). There is the principle of dichotomy of control where a person knows that some things are in our control and others are not. It is, however, our responsibility to ensure that our actions are carried out with virtue throughout our lives.

Researchers initially believed that empathy and kindness aren't seen in children until the second year of life. Karen Wynn and Kiley Hamlin showed that children prefer those who are helpful and kind. Israelis Ronit Roth-Hanania at The Academic

College of Tel Aviv-Yaffo and Maayan Davidov at The Hebrew University of Jerusalem, and Carolyn Zahn-Waxler at the University of Wisconsin, looked at whether empathy might actually be evident at an earlier age. They went into the homes of thirty-seven mostly white, middle and upper-middle class infants from eight to sixteen months and set up three distressing situations:

- The mother pretended to hit her finger with a toy hammer. She was upset for one minute and avoided eye contact with her child so as to not bias the child's response.
- The mother walked towards the baby and pretended to knock her knee showing distress for one minute and without making eye contact.
- The baby was shown a video of another baby crying for one minute.

All the infants showed genuine empathy and feelings of concern for their mothers' pain. The babies tried to work out what had happened, they looked at the hurt body part up to the mother's face and back. Some even made questioning sounds.[11] All these studies suggest that we are born with a capacity for empathic awareness and altruism. In other words, we are born with the ability to be kind.

Cultivating kindness

Many early learning centres and schools are keen to encourage a culture of empathy and kindness. They are aware that this is something that can be cultivated and developed in children and is included in many curriculums.[12] There is a belief that any school-based kindness education programmes support the social-emotional development of children and can even improve school climate.[13]

It can be considered as a moral imperative, a biological reflex and even a necessary behaviour to ensure survival. Whatever your viewpoint, kindness is a sign of a healthy society and a highly desired trait in one another. The idea of valuing and cultivating kindness through society has been illustrated through events such as National Kindness Day and the Pay it Forward movement. Whether or not we are born with a higher level of kindness than someone else, we can still cultivate kindness.

In Dr Lee Rowland's 2018 paper on the psychology of kindness he says, 'Cultivating and extending kindness is an important step in creating a kinder society. Once goodness is established in social networks, the potential for prosocial behaviours and emotions to spread exists.'[14] He calls kindness 'the golden chain' – a phrase, as we read earlier, used by the German writer and statesman Johann Wolfgang von Goethe.

Researchers David Canter, Donna Youngs and Miroslava Yaneva explored what kindness is as they felt that there was no clear definition or distinct measure for it.[15] As part of their work, they developed a framework for kindness which is a forty-item self-report questionnaire which they called the 'kindness measure'. They completed a study using the questionnaire on 165 people differing in age, gender and occupation. They found that there are three distinct aspects of kindness: Benign Tolerance (BT), Empathetic Responsivity (ER), and Principled Proaction (PP). Despite these different types of kindness, they identified a more fundamental form of kindness which they called Core Kindness (CK). Other researchers such as Oliver Curry, Adam Phillips and Barbara Taylor call it 'basic kindness'.[16] [17] Curry does however suggest kindness can have different motivations, including altruism, mutualism, reciprocal altruism and competitive altruism.

Phillips and Taylor also suggest that kindness is connected to complex networks of other concepts such as sympathy, empathy, benevolence, generosity and compassion. They also suggest that it is rooted in the concept of human interdependency. Dr David Hamilton, mentioned earlier, says in his book about kindness, 'the human body is wired for kindness'.[18] He suggests that despite what you might have been told, we're not inherently selfish, we are wired to be kind.

What motivates us?

Thomas Hobbes was an English philosopher, scientist and historian who tried to explain away kindness, arguing that it's not an original or natural moral emotion and source of motivation. He suggests that there must be self-interested motives at work that explain acts of kindness. This is now called 'egoistic psychology' and is the basis of the 'rational economic man' used in economics. Hobbes suggests that kindness is needed for moral motivation and social relations. Moral motivation or normative motivation suggests that our normative judgements have some motivating force.

Motivation is the process that initiates and implements goal-orientated behaviours. It is what causes us to act in a certain way, whether it is about the time we get up in the morning or when we go to bed. Motivation involves biological, emotional, social and cognitive factors that inform and lead to our behaviour. This is different for everyone. What motivates me is not necessarily what motivates you.

I came to know Jesus when I was 14 years old. Up to that point in my life I had always believed in God and tried to live a good life. I thought I could earn my place in heaven. I am sure a lot of people believe the same. People are motivated to be kind and do good works to earn their place in heaven.

In an interview with *The New York Times*, the former New York mayor Michael Bloomberg reflected on his legacy of gun safety, fighting obesity and smoking cessation. Bloomberg said, 'I am telling you if there is a God, when I get to heaven I'm not stopping to be interviewed. I am heading straight in. I have earned my place in heaven. It's not even close.'[19]

The challenge is that as Christians we know that we don't get to heaven because we are good or because of our good deeds. We can never earn our place in heaven. Our motivation to do good deeds and be kind should not be to gain eternal life.

Isaiah 64:6 says:

> All of us have become like one who is unclean, and all our righteous acts are like filthy rags; we all shrivel up like a leaf, and like the wind our sins sweep us away.

Hebrews 11:6 says:

> And without faith it is impossible to please God, because anyone who comes to him must believe that he exists and that he rewards those who earnestly seek him.

Few of us are kind by nature all the time. I certainly do not have an unlimited supply of kindness. There are times when even the best of us can get compassion fatigue. There are also times when we can be really mean. I know because I have been there. I think we can only be truly kind if we learn from the one who is always kind, and allow God's Spirit to change our lives. His love and mercy should motivate us. There are an estimated seventy-two verses about kindness in the Bible. Jesus' life epitomises a kind life and there are countless examples of Jesus demonstrating kindness to people throughout Scripture.

God's mercy and love should motivate us

We may be kind because we are altruistic or want people's praise. The Bible teaches us, however, to be kind because of God's love and mercy to us. This is what should motivate kindness.

- Be kind to one another, tender-hearted, forgiving one another, as God in Christ forgave you. (Eph. 4:32, ESV)
- Offer hospitality to one another without grumbling. (1 Pet. 4:9)
- Let brotherly love continue. Do not neglect to show hospitality to strangers, for thereby some have entertained angels unawares. (Heb. 13:1–2, ESV)
- Finally, all of you, have unity of mind, sympathy, brotherly love, a tender heart, and a humble mind. Do not repay evil for evil or reviling for reviling, but on the contrary, bless, for to this you were called, that you may obtain a blessing. For 'Whoever desires to love life and see good days, let him keep his tongue from evil and his lips from speaking deceit; let him turn away from evil and do good; let him seek peace and pursue it. For the eyes of the Lord are on the righteous, and his ears are open to their prayer. But the face of the Lord is against those who do evil.' (1 Pet. 3:8, ESV)
- Put on then, as God's chosen ones, holy and beloved, compassionate hearts, kindness, humility, meekness, and patience, bearing with one another and, if one has a complaint against another, forgiving each other; as the Lord has forgiven you, so you also must forgive. And above all these put on love, which binds everything together in perfect harmony. (Col. 3:12–14, ESV)

It's a tall order. No one can live like this all the time. The only person who has always been kind is Jesus. He was kind to the woman at the well when no one else would help her or speak to her (John 4). He had dinner with people who were considered the worst of society – see Matthew 9:10. He touched people considered unclean and unsafe as they had the very contagious disease, leprosy. He reached out and touched the sick, the lonely, the afflicted. He sat with older people and children. Never once did he push people away or say he was too tired to see them. He fed the hungry, helped the poor and recognised that people were made in his Father's image. He did not exclude the disabled, was not racist and did not belittle those who were refugees. He taught us that he had no time for social stereotypes. He even forgave those who hurt him. He taught his disciples to do the same. When his Spirit anointed his disciples and filled the early church, his followers were known for their kindness to one another and to those in need.

What if we were all kinder to each other?

Margaret Mead, the American cultural anthropologist is alleged to have said, 'Never doubt that a small group of thoughtful, committed citizens can change the world: indeed, it's the only thing that ever has.'[20] I think that in our fast-changing world, people at times seem to be less generous, more easily offended, more aggressive and don't listen to each other. The Australia Talks National Survey suggests that we are more selfish than we used to be and need to become more kind.[21] This was a study of more than 54,000 people in Australia who were asked to share their thoughts and feelings on almost 500 individual questions.

Kim Baskerville and colleagues in their article about reactions to acts of random kindness suggest that in our fast-paced modern world we are encouraged to think about ourselves rather than other people.[22] They suggest that we have forgotten how to be kind to strangers for the sheer pleasure of helping a fellow human being. Certainly, people are very sceptical when strangers perform random acts of kindness. They expect a catch, think it's a scam and don't think it's an act of kindness.

Why are we so surprised when someone is kind to us? In their study, Kim Baskerville gave 122 people a flower and considered their reactions. They found that women responded more positively to kindness than did men. People responded more positively to kindness when the giver was white, regardless of the race of the receiver. In general people were surprised by the act of kindness. I think it is a shame that they were so surprised. I lived in rural Scotland for part of my later childhood. There was a strong community spirit and neighbours helped each other out. My parents would often be given boxes of vegetables to feed the hungry family or offered fresh lamb for the freezer. My dad would offer practical help in return. He was an all-rounder when it came to things that needed to be fixed. It really impacted me. I have always tried to live a kind life as I wanted to be like the people I grew up with. I know I don't often get it right, but I try.

What would happen if we were all kinder to each other? Would it wipe out hunger, poverty, inequality and illiteracy? Imagine if we all saw people the same, made in God's image. There would be no issues about people who look incredibly different from others. Maybe if we were all a little kinder, our hearts would grow a little bit wider. It's a big ask – maybe we can start with small acts of kindness like giving a bunch of flowers to a lonely neighbour or a smile and a thank you to a busy shop assistant.

We all have a natural level of kindness that we can nurture and grow. It is like an echo or shadow of who we were meant to be, made in the image of God.

Practical pointers

Read Genesis 1:26–27. Consider what it says – that we are made in God's likeness and his image. Consider the full impact of the fractured relationship with God that resulted after the Fall.

Read John 3:16.

> For God so loved the world that he gave his one and only Son, that whoever believes in him shall not perish but have eternal life.

Now, reflect on 2 Corinthians 5:17:

> Therefore, if anyone is in Christ, the new creation has come: the old has gone, the new is here!

Accepting the forgiveness that God gives us through Jesus changes our lives, and we are a new creation. We reflect that in our lives. No longer is kindness an echo of who we were. It is a gift that we are given by God.

How can you be a kinder person?

Summary

There has been a long-standing debate about nature or nurture. Are we born with the code to be kind in our

DNA or is this something that is nurtured because of our home environment or the community we are a part of? I think we are all born with a level of kindness. We may also be motivated to be kinder people by altruism and egoism, or we may think it earns us extra credit to get to heaven. The Bible teaches us that all the things we do will not help us enter heaven; this is only through belief in Jesus Christ, in his death and resurrection (Isa. 64:6; Eph. 2:8–9). Christians believe that kindness can be grown as a fruit of the Spirit. Our prayer for this book is that you will allow this fruit to grow in you.

Prayer

Father,

Thank you that you showed great love to us even though we did not know you.

Thank you that we can know you through the sacrifice of your Son.

Help us to develop the fruit of kindness in our lives. We know that our lives are broken and marked by sin. We also know that your Spirit lives in us if we trust in you. We ask that you will help us grow kindness in our lives.

In Jesus' name.

Amen.

9

Creating a Kindness Culture

Cathy Le Feuvre

I do not pretend to give such a Sum; I only lend it to you. When you . . . meet with another honest Man in similar Distress, you must pay me by lending this Sum to him; enjoining him to discharge the Debt by a like operation, when he shall be able, and shall meet with such another opportunity. I hope it may thus go thro' many hands, before it meets with a Knave that will stop its Progress. This is a trick of mine for doing a deal of good with a little money.

Benjamin Franklin, in a letter to Benjamin Webb.[1]

Suspended kindness

Have you ever had a *caffè sospeso*?

It's a cup of coffee – but one that is very special.

Translated literally from the Italian, *caffè sospeso* means 'suspended coffee' or 'pending coffee' and it's a tradition which originated in the working class cafés of Naples in southern Italy.[2]

It's a drink already paid for, as an act of kindness for a stranger, and if we're thinking about how we can create a kinder culture, it's this sort of initiative – small and insignificant as it might appear – that could well help us build that world we imagine.

We've already read how kindness has become a real buzzword in our twenty-first-century culture, even more so during the pandemic. It feels like everyone has suddenly 'discovered' kindness and the impact it can have on ourselves and on others. There are all kinds of initiatives which are grabbing the imagination of millions of people, and one of them is the popular concept of paying it forward, which we have already spoken of in this book. This is the idea that you do something kind for someone else without even knowing the recipient. You do this maybe because you feel fortunate or because you've been inspired by a kind thing that's been done for you.

All this is nothing new. There's evidence that 'pay it forward' was actually first chronicled back before the birth of Jesus Christ, in ancient Greece in the year 317 BC. It was a key storyline in a prize-winning comedy play in that year entitled *Dyskolos* (loosely translated as 'The Grouch' or 'The Bad-Tempered Man'). It was penned by the ancient Greek playwright Menander and although the play was lost for thousands of years it was recovered and republished in 1957.[3]

Back to that cup of coffee

According to Michele Sergio, the third generation of his family to run the rather famous Gran Caffè Gambrinus, a bar located next to the historic Piazza del Plesbiscito in Naples, *caffè sospeso* is a deep-rooted 'ancient and generous'[4] Neapolitan tradition which dates from around the time of the Unification of Italy in 1861. According to Michele, a well-known connoisseur of all things Neapolitan called Luciano De Crescenzo 'happily grasped the spirit of suspended coffee' and said of the custom:

> When a Neapolitan is happy for some reason, he decides to offer a coffee to a stranger because it is as if he were offering a coffee to the rest of the world.[5]

Those nineteenth-century residents of Naples recognised that when something good had happened to them, maybe they'd had a lucky break and had a bit of money to spare, one of the things they could do was to share that good fortune with someone else. But to choose to make that 'someone' a complete stranger is astonishingly generous. That's what we might call in Christian terms 'servant living'.

The great news is that the concept of 'suspended coffee' didn't remain in Italy. What began in those coffee shops and stalls in Naples is now a global phenomenon. Coffee shop chains, cafés and restaurants around the world are signed up to help people reach out to others with this practical expression of caring and kindness. You can pay for a coffee for anyone that wants to claim it, whether that's someone who can't afford to pay for a drink or just the next one in line at the coffee counter who, when they reach for their purse, is told 'No charge . . . it's a *caffè sospeso*!'

In 2020 during the pandemic in Italy, which was one of the first countries badly hit by the coronavirus, 'suspended coffee' received another injection of enthusiasm as a result of the economic hardships being experienced by so many people during lockdown.

There's even a day dedicated to the custom – 10 December is now, internationally, recognised as 'Suspended Coffee Day'. And, interestingly, this coincides with the United Nations Human Rights Day,[6] also marked annually on 10 December.

Inspired by the phenomenon in Italy, a 'Suspended Coffees' Facebook page was set up in 2013 which, as of the end of 2021, has more than half a million followers. It was created by John Sweeney, who is described as 'founder and chief kindness officer of the Suspended Coffee movement'.[7] What a great title!

As the Facebook page states, 'It's about more than the coffee',[8] and the page is now a place not only to encourage people to buy a drink for others as an 'anonymous' act of kindness, but also a site where people share encouraging messages and thoughts to help others through challenging and stressful times. It's a kind place in a sometimes harsh world.

Caffè sospeso is just part of that Pay It Forward movement which we heard a little about earlier and has become increasingly popular. The phrase, thought to be first coined in the early twentieth century, was in a novel by Lily Hardy Hammond. She was a Christian writer who wrote mostly about social issues, including those related to women. She is considered to be one of the voices of the Social Gospel Movement in the USA in the late nineteenth and early twentieth century, writing about subjects which were, at the time, considered controversial – issues like interracial justice, racial discrimination, poverty and inequalities in the labour market. Social problems, she believed, should be viewed through the lens of Christian principles.[9]

Inspiring a kinder world

In her 1916 book entitled *In the Garden of Delight*, Lily Hardy Hammond wrote: 'You don't pay love back; you pay it forward.'[10] That passing play on words, which captures the spirit of repaying kindness shown to us to people other than the person who was kind to us, has a century later become an iconic phrase much used these days. And it's growing all the time. The best place to see the evidence and be inspired is online. Earlier, we mentioned the Pay It Forward Foundation – its stated mission is 'Inspiring a Kinder World'.[11] This group was founded by the award-winning American novelist and short-story writer Catherine Ryan Hyde, to whom we were introduced earlier in this book. She wrote the novel *Pay it Forward*, which was adapted into a movie of the same name, as you may recall. The film, released in the year 2000, is set in the American city of Las Vegas and tells the story of an 11-year-old boy who is set a school assignment to come up with an idea that will change the world. He decides to do something nice for three people, and then the idea is that those three do something good for another three people . . . it's the start of a goodwill movement known as 'pay it forward'.[12]

Now, you might be wondering why I'm going into a bit of detail about these popular movements. Well, it's because if we are to create a kinder society and kinder communities, and to have kindness just as an integral part of our being and culture, then we do need to engage with the wider society, and these days one of the best ways of doing that is through popular entertainment routes and social media.

I wonder if Lily Hardy Hammond realised that those few words in one of her books would be making such an impact more than a century later. *In the Garden of Delight* is now quoted liberally and is considered by scholars as being 'culturally important, part of the knowledge base of civilization as we know it'.[13]

In an interesting essay entitled 'An Epidemic of Kindness' and published online by the Carolina College of Biblical Studies, the Revd Chris Dickerson references the movie *Pay It Forward* and he makes some pertinent points which I think are worth repeating. At the centre of this interesting article is this question: if we were to all pay forward the kindnesses extended to us, would our world be changed, and quickly?

His answer is a big thumbs up.

> Would our world be a better place if we were simply nice to one another? Would we have better relationships in our families if we

decided to show kindness to our spouse and our kids? Would the workplace be a better environment if co-workers made a choice to show kindness? With a resounding yes, the more important question is heard: How? Kindness is an action, it's something we do.[14]

Five steps to make the world a kinder place

Revd Dickerson takes us through five steps which he believes will make the world a kinder place. But these steps, I think, also help us to highlight those issues which might prevent us building a kinder community.

First, kindness always 'takes the initiative', 'Kindness takes the first step'.[15] We shouldn't wait for others to be kind to us before we do the same to others. We shouldn't wait for someone to say sorry before we ask for their forgiveness if we've fallen out. That might mean we need to show humility and suck up a bit of pride, to risk losing face, but if we take the first step, that's a real sign of kindness.

Second, kindness always has the right incentive. What's that all about? Well, Revd Dickerson explains that in a world where many people make decisions and act based on what they think they will get out of a situation, kindness has to be more empathetic than that. Rather than asking ourselves, 'How will this benefit me?' or 'If I do this kind thing, I wonder what I will get out of it?', the imperative is to be kind without strings attached.

That sounds countercultural to me, in a world where often we are encouraged to win and be successful, even if it means others are disadvantaged. But as Revd Dickerson points out, 'That is the opposite of kindness. Kindness acts out of love. Kindness acts not out of what it gets but out of what it gives.'[16] Earlier, we read about how Jesus broke some of the social rules of his day when he extended his hand of kindness and love. Today some of the rules our culture sets us – me first, profit and success at all costs, status is everything, to name just a few – are those which we may need to turn on their heads if we are to become a kinder culture.

Third on Revd Dickerson's list of steps to make us a kinder people: 'Kindness always is inclusive.' It's not just for those who we like or are like us. He writes: 'Kindness is an action that is no respecter of persons. Kindness says, "You and I are different. But I choose to be nice to you no matter how different we are" . . . Kindness should not exclude anyone.'[17]

If we're to create a truly kinder society, one where – as we've read earlier – kindness is part of our breathing and being, this might be the one which is hardest, because the natural inclination is for us to be kind to people who are approachable, to those who are like us. What about strangers who we've never met and who might look and live very differently to us? What about those people we don't like, who've hurt us? What about those people who, maybe, have ridiculed us for our faith?

It would be so easy just to retaliate to negativity, to be nasty back to those who treat us poorly. But will that create a good working environment? No. Will that create a kinder world? No.

I've spent my life working in the British media and broadcasting industry and the fact that I've never hidden that I'm a Christian hasn't always gone down well with colleagues. When I was a young reporter, I was often laughed at, especially as I am a non-drinker and a non-smoker in a world which often revolved around socialising and the pub. I think I was certainly seen as a bit of an oddity. Later there were times when I know for sure I was disadvantaged because of the perception would-be employers might have had about what a person like me could bring to a team. I won't say I was persecuted because that's a much more harmful and sinister concept, but I certainly felt that my faith was a bit of a challenge to some of those

I worked with. And that was surprising and disappointing because, although I never hid the fact that I was a Christian, I never 'rammed it down people's throats'. For me, being a person of faith in the workplace was about being quietly faithful and ensuring that people around me, those in my team, especially younger colleagues, could find me helpful, trustworthy and yes, kind.

If you're wondering, all this didn't stop me having a fantastic career, one which took me to many fascinating places and introduced me to many wonderful people. While I may never have reached the dizzy heights of success or earned the huge wads of money that some of my erstwhile colleagues were privileged to enjoy, or which might be seen as the pinnacle of success in the industry, as a storyteller I was privileged to talk with hundreds of people who were kind enough to help me share their stories and that was, and still is, an honour.

Many times down the years I have turned to the words of Jesus to help me through tricky situations:

> A new command I give you: love one another. As I have loved you, so you must love one another.
>
> *John 13:34*

And if that's not enough encouragement, how about the biblical imperative which encourages us not just to be kind to those who despise us, who maybe choose unkindness towards us, but actually to do more than that?

> But to you who are listening I say: love your enemies, do good to those who hate you, bless those who curse you, pray for those who ill-treat you. If someone slaps you on one cheek, turn to them the other also. If someone takes your coat, do not withhold your shirt from them. Give to everyone who asks you, and if anyone takes

what belongs to you, do not demand it back. Do to others as you would have them do to you.

Luke 6:27–31

We're right back at that Golden Rule again. Perhaps that really is the answer to creating a kinder world.

Revd Chris Dickerson's essay 'An Epidemic of Kindness' has a fourth step to building a kinder world: 'Kindness always has the right intensity.'[18] I think what he's getting at here is that being kind is not just a token gesture, it's not something we do to tick a box or two and make ourselves feel good: 'Kindness is not minimal living. It is not a decision to see how little I can do for someone else. Kindness is a choice to do all that we can for all those we can. Kindness has the right intensity when it gives its all for the other person.'[19]

It's the kindness of spirit which is just part of our nature. It's determined; we do it without thinking; just as Jesus lived kindness, so we are encouraged to do the same. But it's not just a duty as a Christian. We choose this way of life, turning our back on what might be our natural inclinations to criticise and offer sarcasm and cynicism.

Finally, Revd Dickerson believes that kindness 'always becomes infective'. It's contagious. When we are kind, or nice to people, it encourages them to be kind to others.

To build a kinder world, we need to understand that people learn by example. Just as parents and adults who have children in their lives understand that young people will often behave well, or badly, if they see the adults around them behaving in that way, so people will learn from our behaviours towards others. We may not even know they are watching, listening and learning . . . but I believe if people see kindness, they may be inclined to be more kind in their own motivations and actions.

As we realise the love and kindness that our heavenly Father and his Son Jesus have extended to us, so we are encouraged to be kind to each other. To pay it forward, if you like. Revd Dickerson has something to say about this as well:

> The same is true of the kindness of God. The Bible says, 'God demonstrates His own love toward us, in that while we were yet sinners, Christ died for us' (Romans 5:8). God took the initiative to show kindness to humanity. He did it for our sake. He does not exclude anyone, as long as they come by way of the cross of Jesus Christ. He did not hold anything back.[20]

So, it's all possible. If we all followed the example of Jesus, what I called earlier in this book the 'Jesus Kindness' way, then we're on the road to a kinder world.

Of course, not everyone is a Jesus person, or even a person of faith, and we have learned that kindness isn't confined to those of us who profess a faith. There's also a suggestion that kindness comes naturally to all of us, and that kindness will help elevate our human culture. So, let's live with hope.

I'm encouraged that the idea of being kind seems to have captivated millions of people and that it's being recognised as a way of making a difference in many areas of life.

An anti-bullying campaign

Take the Anti-Bullying Alliance in England and Wales, for example. Their theme for Anti-Bullying Week from 15–19 November 2021 was 'One Kind Word'. After living through the height of the COVID-19 pandemic, it was a word which really resonated with many of those with whom the alliance works. The theme was chosen because of a direct result of what the younger generation and others felt would make a difference to bullying. Their website explained it this way:

> Following the success of the campaign in 2020 – when a jaw-dropping 80% of schools marked the week reaching over 7.5 million children and young people – the Anti-Bullying Alliance (which coordinates the campaign each year in England and Wales) asked over 400 young people, teachers, and parents, what they wanted from Anti-Bullying Week 2021. Again and again, the young and not-so-young told us they wanted anti-bullying work to be about hope and the positive and kind things we can do to halt hurtful behaviour in its tracks.[21]

A kind spirit

But is 'being kind' and 'not being hurtful' enough to change behaviours in a school, and in a whole community and an entire world? Here are a few suggestions which the Anti-Bullying Alliance believe can help. And this list is their 'call to action'. It's stuff we've read about before . . . but it's worth reminding ourselves of the impact that a kind spirit can have.

> Ask if someone's OK. Say you're sorry. Just say hey.
>
> In a world that can sometimes feel like it's filled with negativity, one kind word can provide a moment of hope. It can be a turning point. It can change someone's perspective. It can change their day. It can change the course of a conversation and break the cycle of bullying.
>
> Best of all, one kind word leads to another. Kindness fuels kindness. So from the playground to Parliament, and from our phones to our homes, together, our actions can fire a chain reaction that powers positivity.
>
> It starts with one kind word. It starts today.[22]

So, what's stopping us? Why isn't everyone embracing this new, kinder world?

Well, we know that not everyone will get it, for all sorts of reasons. Selfishness, personal ambition, lack of empathy, a misunderstanding of other people and their needs, an unwillingness to understand people who are 'different', the drive to succeed and make loads of money.

If we are to create a kinder world, then surely that can't just be about individuals doing 'kind stuff' for each other, in church, through charities, even feeling inspired to pay it forward by leaving a coffee for someone else in our local coffee shop.

It has to be bigger than that – it has to touch every aspect of our culture, including business.

Capitalism, which is the overriding economic and political model in the world today, is where trade and industry are controlled by private owners for profit, rather than by the state for more general benefit. And with the need for 'profit' can come the inevitable – people putting themselves and their bank balances ahead of the needs of others, including the workers who make the products we sell: that 'me first' culture which some might have us believe is the only way to success. Well, even in the world of commerce, finance, business and industry, some are beginning to think that there might be another way and we can find lots of research and papers online to that effect.

One that caught my attention was an article published in May 2021 in the *Harvard Business Review* by Ovul Sezer, Kelly Nault and Nadav Klein which encourages readers not to completely rule out kindness in business. The title – 'Don't Underestimate the Power of Kindness at Work'[23] says it all, really.

The paper is written through the lens of the experience of a year of global pandemic, a time when many workplaces were physically empty, people met online and there was little interaction between colleagues. No opportunities for people to smile at each other in the corridor or to spontaneously say 'good job' when someone had just made a great presentation.

The paper includes some suggestions for this ongoing way of working, because we know that even when the COVID-19 pandemic is over its worst, experts predict these new working regimes will persist. We've all learned that we are able to work productively from home, maybe don't have to travel every day into the office and be under the boss's nose. The 'remote' way of working has turned traditional working practice on its head, and although not every business will find it practicable in the future and some business owners and leaders may be concerned that this 'new way' will adversely affect them and their bottom line, the *HBR* researchers have an answer to that dilemma: 'We offer a humble suggestion: Kindness. This past year, most management advice has focused on how to sustain productivity during the pandemic, yet the power of kindness has been largely overlooked. Practicing kindness by giving compliments and recognition has the power to transform our remote workplace.'[24]

Their conclusion is that 'organizations benefit from actively fostering kindness. In workplaces where acts of kindness become the norm, the spillover effects can multiply fast. When people receive an act of kindness, they pay it back, research shows – and not just to the same person, but often to someone entirely new. This leads to a culture of generosity in an organization.'[25]

I think back to that research undertaken at the Coca-Cola plant in Madrid which we heard about in chapter six, where kindness in the workplace grew exponentially as a result of some of the workers being asked to deliberately be kind to their colleagues.

The *Harvard Business Review* authors also present research-backed benefits of kindness to back up their theory that kindness can enhance a business. They reference a study which analysed 3,500 businesses employing more than 50,000 individuals,[26] where researchers found that 'acts of courtesy, helping, and praise were related to core goals of organizations. Higher rates of these behaviours were predictive of productivity, efficiency, and lower turnover rates. When leaders and employees act kindly towards each other, they facilitate a culture of collaboration and innovation.'[27]

A happy workforce

A happy workforce will be a more productive and efficient workforce? Now that's a thought!

But how to start? The team have another suggestion: 'People are naturally sensitive to the behaviours of high-status team members. By giving compliments and praising their employees, leaders are likely to motivate team members to copy their behaviour and create norms of kindness in teams.'[28] This is all sounding familiar, isn't it? People leading by example? Even if they're working remotely kindness can be part of the deal: 'Leaders can set aside time during Zoom meetings for a "kindness round" in which team members are free to acknowledge each other's work. This need not take much time – even a few minutes a week will suffice. But these few minutes can boost morale and social connection, especially when months-long projects are mostly completed over Zoom.'[29]

Now, that's a great idea! And it works not just virtually but in person as well, and not just in the business context. Positive feedback and encouragement work in all contexts. Church meetings where you don't just rush through the agenda (including the prayers at the start and end) but give time to listen – really listen – to each other. How about a political structure where, rather than opposing politicians and parliamentarians spending time and effort to pick holes in each other's policies, motivation and practice, they just tried to work together, to encourage each other for the better good of society? I know many might think this is 'pie in the sky', but how would it appear if we all began to work more collaboratively? What might that do to the partisan cultures we've grown up with, the structures with which we're accustomed? The more cynical among us, and those who believe that human culture depends on a certain amount of conflict, might think that a community where we are all 'nice' to each other could make life rather boring.

But if we are to truly create a kinder world, we need to address some of the toxicity which exists in our systems and culture, and being kind to each other doesn't mean we can't have differing opinions and approaches to life. Being kind doesn't mean a lack of robust argument. It may mean, however, a little more grace as we learn to work through our difference.

We have a very long way to go, that's for certain, and it might all seem rather daunting, especially in a world where much of our human interaction and influencing is not even face-to-face. But we have to start somewhere, as the *Harvard Business Review* article concludes:

'The power of kindness can mitigate the ill effects of our increasingly online social world. It is an essential leadership skill that can cascade through people, changing the culture of the workplace along the way.'[30]

Changing the culture. That's what it's about. If we are to create a kindness culture, it's not just about the doing but also about the being.

Being kind, showing kindness and consideration, being nice to people – which doesn't have to mean not being strong and forthright, or standing up for what we believe to be true and important. Remember Professor Barry H. Corey's book *Love Kindness: Discover the Power of a Forgotten Christian Virtue* from chapter three? Being kind isn't to be bland. Sometimes it's to be daring, to step outside the norms and expectations of our times.

Imagine a world where business, politics, education, church, media, sport and interpersonal relationships were built first and foremost on the principles of kindness. Taking other people's views into account, encouraging and praising each other rather than always attempting to get the upper hand, to show the other person's weaknesses, trying to score points off each other.

It seems an impossible task. But if we can't change the whole world, maybe we can start with our own life.

Yes, it might just start with developing a habit of paying it forward or leaving a coffee for a stranger next time we go out to buy our daily cappuccino or latte. It might just be a smile for a colleague, or doing the tea round at work, if we're in work. Or finding things to praise in others when we're in those interminable online work meetings.

It might be small steps, one day at a time, and it may require a change of heart for some of us. It might take sacrifice, biting our tongue when a cruel word is about to come out of our mouths. Learning to be kind may be a lifetime's work.

Practical pointers

Here are some things you can do if you want to make a start building a kinder world:

- Don't judge people too quickly. We never know what's going on in their lives.
- Be patient. Find time and space to learn from others.
- Try to listen to people . . . it's called empathy.
- Kindness rubs off on others – maybe we need to lead by example.
- Forget the cynicism. If we are to build a kindly world, we need to shrug off our natural inclination to want always to have the upper hand in our business dealings, relationships and even our church.
- And smile. It really makes a difference. It changes our mood and it can lift another person's day and change their world.

Summary

As we've looked at some of the initiatives which have helped people to express kindness, I hope we've learned a few things about building a kindness culture. This might not immediately change the whole world, but it could change the world we live in.

Prayer

Lord God,

Help us to start to envisage a new culture, a new world, where kindness is at the heart. Inspire us and challenge us to be the difference you want us to be in our communities, in our families, in our places of work, sports clubs, political debates, schools and churches. Give us opportunities for even small kindnesses and help us every day to grow a spirit of kindliness and positivity so that we may, with your help, begin to change our world, our culture . . . one act of kindness at a time, one day at a time.

Amen.

10

Living Out Kindness: Looking to the Future

Debbie Duncan

We love because he first loved us.

1 John 4:19

Throughout this book, Cathy and I have discussed, analysed, and illustrated the importance of kindness in our own lives and those around us. You have heard stories from many different places about how kindness has changed things.

One of our key questions was this: are we born with innate kindness? Our response has been: Yes. We were made in God's image and our lives carry the echo of what would have been that perfect life until the Fall. This was when humankind turned from God, disobeying him and breaking down our relationship with him. We have also learned that we respond to kindness because God first showed great kindness to us (see 1 John 4:19).

Kindness is an explosive, extraordinary vortex of a word that encompasses everything from sympathy and empathy, to sensitivity and compassion. Kindness also cannot be faked. The amazing part of this journey is that not only has God shown us great kindness but he also wants us to live our best lives, mirroring the qualities of Jesus.

So how do we do that? We allow his Spirit to dwell within us – growing this precious fruit.

Can we all be kind?

Dr Lee Rowland says:

> The beauty of kindness is that it is open to anyone. We can all opt to choose kindness if we wish. It is free, easily accessible to rich and poor alike, and is universally understood. Thus, if it turns out that simple acts of everyday kindness can send ripple effects of wellbeing through society, then promoting and facilitating that has to be a constructive pursuit.[1]

What Rowland is saying is that kindness changes people and society. It is a gift that is within all of us. I would like to think that we are all 'human-kind'. Sometimes we live with the wrong idea that the fruits of the Spirit are found only within those who are in faith communities. You don't need to have faith to be kind. Think of all the stories we have heard throughout this book.

In Acts 28 we learn about one of Paul's missionary journeys. On this occasion he had been shipwrecked on his way to Rome. Paul and other passengers and crew were cast ashore in Malta, just south of Sicily. It was initially thought that St Paul's Bay and St Paul's Island were where they were shipwrecked but nowadays it is believed that the prevalent north-easterly winds led them to an area known as Il-Munxar, which has a submerged reef and a sandy beach near St Thomas Bay in the south-eastern part of Malta.

Luke, the writer of Acts, tells us: 'Once safely on shore, we found out that the island was called Malta. The islanders showed us unusual kindness. They built a fire and welcomed us all because it was raining and cold' (Acts 28:1–2).

Matthew Henry in his commentary on Acts 28 explains that they were barbarous people because 'they did not, in language and customs, conform either to the Greeks or Romans, who looked (superciliously enough) upon all but themselves as barbarians, though otherwise civilized enough, and perhaps in some cases more civil than they. These barbarous people, however they were called so, were full of humanity.'[2]

It's not a nice description and it's speaking more of the culture at the time of writing. Henry is not being disparaging as 'barbarous' is the word translated from the original manuscripts of the Bible.

You can, however, get the gist of what Henry is saying. They were not what the Greeks or Romans considered 'civilised' and they surprised them all as they were so kind.

I think it would be good to point out that at times the Greek and Roman cultures were far from kind. A 1,200-year history of an evolved, civilised Roman culture, and they still followed the whim of Caesar even when he demanded the desolation and slaughter of innocents. The Romans were not known for their great kindness – unlike the people of Malta.

I would like the society I live in to be kind. I have seen great acts of kindness throughout the COVID-19 pandemic. So why can't we be a little kinder each day and if we were, what would our society look like?

How can we grow kindness in our world?

Writer and speaker Scott Mautz says that we should not just '. . . role-model kindness. Live it as a core value'. He also suggests that it should be a non-negotiable value.[3] The Harvard psychologist and founder of the Harvard Graduate School of Education's kindness and justice project, Richard Weissbourd, highlights the importance of teaching and modelling kindness in children.[4] Certainly, many schools have taken this concept and included it in their curriculum.

In a pluralistic, selfish society driven by technology with an eroded sense of connectedness, empathy, compassion, and kindness have been shown to change things.[5] To do this, kindness should be integrated into areas of our society. We should be teaching it to the young, role-modelling it to neighbours. We should be loving our neighbours as ourselves. A tall order, but we are not doing it alone.

Kindness is a lifestyle

As I write this, we are entering the season of Advent. I love this season – it's the pregnant gap before the rush of Christmas. For many people, it's a season of thankfulness and joy. People seem kinder – handing gifts to neighbours they have hardly spoken to all year or giving the postman a box of chocolates.

Kindness should be a lifestyle. It is not just a seasonal trend. It should be a daily choice of deciding to be kind. As Christians we can rely on God's Spirit to grow the fruit of 'love, joy, peace, forbearance, kindness, goodness, faithfulness, gentleness and self-control' found in Galatians 5:22–23. But fruit takes time to grow. I can't think of any fruit that appears overnight. Some of the fastest-growing fruits are strawberries and raspberries, and even they take about sixty days! Most trees bear fruit after one to two years, although the pawpaw tree takes between five and seven years. You may not have tasted a pawpaw (otherwise known as papaya), but I have been told it's like a cross between a banana and a mango and is like a tropical extravaganza in your mouth. It doesn't travel well so we find it hard to get it in our shops.

Our aim is to grow fruit, robust, life-changing fruit that impacts society. We don't want fruit that is fragile and can't get very far. It may take weeks or years, but we want to keep growing. This fruit should be our default mode where we have a heart of continual service every day.

Wouldn't it be wonderful if we were known for our great kindness? That we were full of humanity and known as being human-kind?

Cathy Le Feuvre

When Debbie asked if I'd like to write another book with her, my knee-jerk reaction was: 'Yes, of course.' I loved the first experience of writing with my friend for several reasons – we have core values and faith which we share, but we come from very different life experiences and perspectives. We also share the same sense of humour, which is always a good thing!

But this time around, things were very different. When we co-wrote *Lifelines*[6] we were in the same space. Near neighbours, we could chat face-to-face regularly and work and laugh together, usually in Debbie's kitchen! In 2020, however, meeting up was impossible thanks to the coronavirus. Yes, online 'chats' helped but, like many friends and co-workers across the globe, we were in different places and different circumstances.

As we wrote this book, the world appeared to be coming out of the worst of the pandemic, but a realisation was dawning that this is a virus, with its many implications – economic, physical, emotional and spiritual – that we will live with for many years. There has, of course, been a good deal of heartache, trauma, challenge and loss, but one thing that seems to have emerged from this pandemic is that people across the globe have recognised again, or for the first time, the need we humans have to be kind to each other and to experience kindness.

The idea of writing a book about kindness had been in Debbie's mind for a while, and she knew I was interested because a change of work circumstances meant that I was, among other things, doing some PR for the Jersey Kindness Festival. As a broadcaster I'd worked with the organiser for a few years and had learned so much about the subject along the way, and now here I was helping with the event. The subject seemed perfect for me.

Kindness is not just an action, it's also a process

Now, if there's one thing I've learned it's that you can never know enough about a subject, and the experience of writing this book has once again taught me that. Through research and reading the Bible and many other sources, and trawling through the internet, I've discovered that kindness might sound simple to achieve but it is much deeper than just 'being nice' and not annoying people. It's a value which, if we take it seriously, has the potential to turn our world upside down.

In fact, I would suggest that if we don't keep learning and working at it, then kindness can easily wane, because although we believe that we are born to be kind, life has a way of intervening. Our culture, which in many instances is self and celebrity-obsessed, image-conscious and always striving towards monetary success, has a habit of dragging us away from those values which we know are good for us and for our communities, but which seem to be 'countercultural'. Plus, kindness is not something we should do just because we get something in return, or because we expect to be rewarded or get a pat on the back.

Neither Debbie nor I profess to be experts in the field, but we have tried to bring you some evidence by cleverer people than us who've done a lot of research and made observations into this subject which is so important, we believe, to the future of the human race. For many people, making kindness part of their everyday life, just as Jesus did, has transformed their lives and the lives of those around them.

We know that when we practise something it becomes, over time, a more natural way of living – exercise and healthy eating are just one example. In our spiritual lives we are encouraged to develop the practice of daily prayer and reading of the Scriptures . . . the more we listen to God, the more we will hear from him. And so, practising kindness might be something we could all think about and cultivate in our own lives. The more we do it, the better we will become at that 'breathing kindness' way of life we read about in this narrative.

We've also learned that people often follow the example of others, so the more kindness we show, the more others may follow. But perhaps it's up to us to start!

Kindness is not just for the pandemic, it's for life

During the pandemic (so far) many millions of people around the globe seem to have discovered the power of kindness for the first time, and that's wonderful. Reaching out a hand of friendship appears to have been a natural human reaction to the difficulties being experienced by their communities and those around them and the outpouring of compassion and kindness, especially during the lockdowns, has been inspirational.

But I suppose the main question in my mind is this: is this kindness just for the pandemic, or for life?

There's much talk about when we go back to normal, or near-normal. Will that mean that the kindnesses we witnessed and experienced will disappear as people return to something resembling normality? When we go back to our busy lives, when people return to employment and there is not so much need for emergency assistance, will kindness vanish? Or might that kindness, which people have experienced in these past years, have made a deeper, long-lasting influence on our thinking and behaviours? Will this be one of the best legacies of the COVID-19 global pandemic?

Being an eternal optimist, I pray that kindness will have made such an impact on our world during this difficult time that it will have taught us something, as individuals, communities and even nations. But, if nothing else, this book and others will have captured some of the essence of the kind world we seem to be living in right now.

And of course, as we've learned, although human kindness has been highlighted during these past few years, it is certainly not new. Kindness is not a modern construct.

Back even before the time of Christ, the Greek storyteller Aesop (c. 620–564 BC) was telling tales, many of which involved animals and had morals embedded in them. They were 'teaching tales', if you like.

In 'The Lion and the Mouse'[7] we hear how a lion threatens to eat a mouse that wakes him from sleep. The mouse begs forgiveness, pointing out that eating such a tiny creature should be above such a noble animal. The mouse is set free but later, when the lion has been captured by hunters, the mouse remembers the kindness and frees the King of the Jungle by gnawing through the ropes of the net in which the lion is imprisoned.

The moral of the story? *'No act of kindness, no matter how small, is ever wasted.'*

In ancient Bible times, before Jesus Christ, and as expressed in the Old Testament, the Hebrew word most used to denote kindness was *chesed*,[8] which among other things means a loyal love which is shown in actions rather than emotions.

The Holman Bible Dictionary describes *chesed* as 'an integral part of covenant relations'[9] – the agreement or contract between people, and between God and humankind. It was reciprocal . . . a good deed deserved another in return. Just as God gives us his loving kindness so we, in return, must extend that to our fellow man, woman and child: the love between people shown in relationships. Although it was originally seen as distinct from compassion, mercy and grace, over time the concepts grew together and then, in the person of Jesus Christ, we see all this in one perfect human being.

If we are to see kindness as part of our culture, embedded deeply in our relationships, then perhaps we do need to see this as part of not just our natural compassion as humans, but because it's the essence of being alive, being part of community – that living together and sharing not just common space but common values.

In Wales there's an International Music Eisteddfod – a musical festival – at a place called Llangollen, and in November 2017 the organisers commissioned a survey to mark World Kindness Day on 13 November. The results revealed a good deal about what people thought about kindness and the way it impacted on them.[10] Asked to quantify acts of kindness, the research showed that the average Brit claimed to do nine acts of kindness each month – more than half of those polled reckoned that they had carried out a good deed in the twenty-four hours before being surveyed. Seven per cent claimed they did thirty-one or more good deeds per month – more than one a day! Impressive!

More important than the self-confessed goodly actions, 83 per cent of people believed that doing a good deed has positive benefits for our mental health. If you remember, Debbie told us about that back in chapter four. But the question is how; what can we do – practically – to make this happen in ourselves and in others?

The Llangollen Eisteddfod survey outlined the top ten Acts of Kindness[11] that make us all happier or happiest, and none of them are beyond you and me adding to our daily life and practices. Here's their helpful list of things which they found make us happiest, with a few minor tweaks here and there from me:

- Listen to someone
- Give a compliment
- Make someone laugh
- Give a hug
- Smile at someone
- Give an unexpected gift
- Give up a seat on public transport for someone who needs it more than you
- Donate unwanted items to charity
- Offer and help to carry another person's shopping
- Donate money

When it comes to the division of the sexes, the 2017 survey showed that there is a gender divide – more than half the women surveyed agreed that undertaking an act of kindness boosted happiness, compared to just a third of men, and there also seemed to be a difference in the understanding of kindness between the age groups.

The group we call millennials (18- to 34-year-olds) were revealed to be the least altruistic – 45 per cent of those surveyed admitted that they performed a simple act of kindness or good deed because they believed that something good would happen to them in return. However, those aged over 55 appeared to be the most selfless group, with only 11 per cent expecting to see any gain from their good deeds.[12] Perhaps that's just the result of life experience.

The Llangollen Eisteddfod survey also revealed some more interesting but disappointing facts about life in the year 2017. Only 7 per cent of people questioned from across the UK said that they felt that people were kinder now than a decade ago, with 44 per cent stating that they felt people were less kind than before.[13]

I wonder, if that survey were to be conducted now, after a couple of years of pandemic, whether there would be different results?

In early autumn 2021, BBC Radio 4 partnered with academics at the University of Sussex on a huge science project aimed at increasing understanding of the role that kindness plays in our lives. By the time this book is published we will know more, including the results of an in-depth online questionnaire that many thousands of people took part in, exploring the role of kindness in our lives.

The Kindness Test is just one piece of study in a field which has grabbed the attention not just of the public and the media, but also academics, including at the University of Sussex in south-east England. According to the university's website, academics there are developing a specialist in the 'science of kindness'. They have created the UK's first-ever academic position dedicated to the psychology of kindness. The website explains the motivation in this way:

> Kindness is an area of research which is rapidly expanding, with neuroscientists examining its impact on the brain, psychologists researching what prompts us to behave kindly – and what can

> prevent us from being kind – and political scientists studying its application to politics.
>
> The pandemic has brought the topic of kindness to the fore, highlighting inspiring examples of true kindness in action, and with thousands joining community WhatsApp groups. The latest research is demonstrating that kindness can be central to success at work, in politics and in relationships.[14]

The Kindness Test and study is headed up by Professor Robin Banerjee, head of the School of Psychology at the University of Sussex and Principal Investigator on the research. They are working alongside BBC Radio 4 broadcaster and Visiting Professor of the Public Understanding of Psychology at the University of Sussex, Claudia Hammond.

Professor Banerjee said that although recent research has begun to tell us more about the powerful impacts of kindness on people and communities, there is so much we still don't know.

> This major survey, led by a team of researchers at the University of Sussex in partnership with the BBC, is designed to help us learn more about kindness in our lives – how people's attitudes and experiences vary across different groups, and how kindness relates to our mental health, well-being, and other social and psychological experiences.[15]

So, we can expect to hear much more about kindness in the future. I hope you agree, that's exciting.

However, my prayer is that it doesn't just become academic, or a part of history related to the global COVID-19 pandemic, but truly personal. I pray that by doing so, kindness infiltrates our culture and begins to alter our motivations in life – our education, work and business, media and communications systems, church and inter-denominational and inter-faith relationships and, of course, our connections and daily interactions with the others who share this planet with us.

As Christians, I pray that we all learn that kindness really is a gift; one that grows out of our ongoing and growing spiritual life with Christ; that we will never take God's kindness to us for granted and that we will, every day, be inspired to share that with our world.

Practical pointers

Throughout this book we have listed a few things along the way which might help us grow in kindness. But before we sign off, if you want to make a start, here are just a few reminders:

- Be intentionally kind every day and consider how you can do it – it may take a little planning, but practise makes perfect.
- Small kindnesses matter – look for opportunities to be kind. You don't have to change the world but if you do something, like phone a lonely person, you will be changing their world.
- Big kindnesses are also important – find ways you can weave and factor and plan kindness into not just your day-to-day behaviour but also into your church, your working life, your commercial and business practices, and leadership.
- Simply smile more – this will raise your spirits and those of the people around you.

- Be kind not just to others, but also to yourself. Don't be overly self-critical; give yourself a break . . . spiritual, emotional and physical.
- Keep a journal of your kindness journey and read it back from time to time to be inspired.

Summary

As we look at the world around us, we can easily be disappointed with what we see. The way people sometimes treat each other with cruelty and heartlessness, often highlighted by the never-ending negative news headlines. Wars and discontent, selfishness, and greed.

But if we are to create a future world where kindness becomes the norm, we need to focus less on the bad and more on the good. Let's look for the light of kindness in our world, celebrate the kindnesses we discover and encourage and applaud those who are kind not just to us but to others.

If we are among those who have felt the spirit of kindness more keenly during the pandemic period, let's determine to ensure that kindness becomes the habit of a lifetime.

If we are people of faith, let's look more closely at the life of Jesus Christ, the pure example of human kindness. Let's seek his guidance to point us in the direction of the kindnesses he would have us do and the lives of people he would have us touch.

And let's ask God's Spirit to help us, to give us that gift of kindness which the world so needs, not just in a global pandemic, but for all time.

Prayer

Lord,
Give us a heart of kindness.
Open our eyes to the needs of others, so that we may be the kindness difference that so many are yearning.
Make us the type of person for whom kindness comes naturally, like breathing.
And, by your Spirit, give us the gift of kindness so your love and compassion and kindness will become known to all who know you and to those who do not recognise you.
Amen.

A Final Reflection on Kindness

Having read these ten chapters, we hope you have a deeper understanding of kindness. We also hope that it has challenged you to be more intentional about being kind.

One way we might consider what we have learned about this important topic is to use reflection. This may help us to bridge the gap between what we are now and where we want to be. It can provide us with the tools to help us grow.

Reflection is a process where we examine our own thoughts and feelings. It can be retrospective, or we can reflect on what is happening in the middle of an event. We do this to take the time to consider what we can learn from these experiences. It is a conversation between thought and action.

It also involves some thinking time, so we need to make sure we have some time and space to do this. But a warning . . . reflection can be challenging. We may relive or review experiences we don't want to remember. I [Debbie] once organised a surprise for someone, and they did not react in the way I expected them to. It was not easy to remember the event later, but I was able to learn something about it once I reflected on it and asked myself some questions about the experience.

Here are some questions you can ask yourself as you reflect on an experience or event. This may be an event when you decided to put into practice what you have learned from this book. You decide to knock on your neighbour's door and ask them for dinner. You stop and talk to the young mother at the school gate. You have never spoken to her before. You cook a meal for someone who you know has been ill and drop it off at their doorstep.

- Describe the event.
- How did it make me feel?
- What went well?
- What didn't go so well?
- What are the key lessons I have learned from this experience?

One way we can structure how we learn is to journal – this is where you write down and record specific events and relate it to experiences, thoughts, feelings and emotions. It's a written record of your journey.

We would recommend that you journal or record your experiences as you try to be more intentional about kindness. You may want to carry out an act of kindness each day and record this journey over the days and weeks that lie ahead. But there are also times in the year when you could focus on this – for instance, you could chart your kindness journey during Lent. It's up to you, really, to find the kindness in yourself and to discover ways to share it with those around you.

Debbie and Cathy

Bibliography

Aknin, L.B., E.W. Dunn, J. Proulx, I. Lok, M.I. Norton, 'Does Spending Money on Others Promote Happiness?: A Registered Replication Report', *Journal of Personality and Social Psychology*, 119(2) (2020) e15–e26.

Anti-bullying Alliance, 'Anti-Bullying Week 2021: One Kind Word' *National Children's Bureau* (2022) www.anti-bullyingalliance.org.uk/anti-bullying-week/anti-bullying-week-2021-one-kind-word (accessed 30 December 2021).

Aristotle (trans. Lee Honeycutt), 'Kindness', *Rhetoric*, Book II, chapter 7. Archived from the original on 13 December 2004, https://web.archive.org/web/20041213221951/http://www.public.iastate.edu/~honeyl/Rhetoric/rhet2-7.html (accessed 30 December 2021).

Ballatt, J., P. Campling, 'Intelligent Kindness: Reforming the Culture of Healthcare' (London: RCPsych Publications, 2011).

Baskerville, K., K. Johnson, E. Monk-Turner, Q. Slone, H. Standley, S. Stansbury . . . J. Young, 'Reactions to Random Acts of Kindness', *The Social Science Journal*, 37(2) (2000) pp. 293–298.

Bloom, P., 'Morality Special: Infant Origins of Human Kindness', *New Scientist*, 208(2782) (2010) pp. 44–45.

Bloom, P., 'The Moral Life of Babies', *New York Times Magazine* (2019) https://www.nytimes.com/2010/05/09/magazine/09babies-t.html (accessed 1 December 2021).

Bregman, Rutger © 2020, Translation © Elizabeth Manton and Erica Moore, 'Humankind: A Hopeful History', Bloomsbury Publishing Plc.

Campling, P., 'Reforming the Culture of Healthcare: The Case for Intelligent Kindness', *BJPsych Bulletin*, 39(1) (2015) pp. 1–5.

Canter, D., D. Youngs, M. Yaneva, 'Towards a Measure of Kindness: An Exploration of a Neglected Interpersonal Trait', *Personality and Individual Differences*, 106 (2017) pp. 15–20.

Carter, C.S., 'Oxytocin Pathways and the Evolution of Human Behaviour', *Annual Review of Psychology*, 65 (2014) pp. 17–39.

Cassell, E., *Oxford Handbook of Positive Psychology* (New York, NY: Oxford University Press, 2009, second edn), pp. 393–403.

Chancellor, J., S. Margolis, K. Jacobs Bao, S. Lyubomirsky, 'Everyday prosociality in the workplace: The reinforcing benefits of giving, getting, and glimpsing', *Emotion* (Washington, DC), 18(4) (2018). Retrieved from https://escholarship.org/uc/item/9t0213nd (accessed 13 January 2022).

Chappet, Marie-Claire, 'How to actually be kind during the Coronavirus pandemic: Let's ensure this sense of community long outlasts the pandemic', *Glamour UK* (2020) www.glamourmagazine.co.uk/article/kindness-in-the-time-of-coronavirus (accessed 30 December 2021).

Cherry, Kendra, 'The Basics of Prosocial Behavior', *Verywell Mind* (2020) www.verywellmind.com/what-is-prosocial-behavior-2795479 (accessed 30 December 2021).

Cole-King, A., P. Gilbert, 'Compassionate Care: The Theory and the Reality', Journal of Holistic Health Care 8(3), (2011), pp. 29–37. http://www.connectingwithpeople.org/sites/default/files/Compassionate%20care%20ACK%20and%20PG.pdf (accessed 1 October 2021).

Corey, Professor Barry H., *Love Kindness: Discover the Power of a Forgotten Christian Virtue* (Wheaton, IL: Tyndale House, Publishers, Inc., 2016).

Curry, O.S., L.A. Rowland, C.J. Van Lissa, S. Zlotowitz, J. McAlaney, H. Whitehouse, 'Happy to Help? A Systematic Review and Meta-analysis of the Effects of Performing Acts of Kindness on the Well-being of the Actor', *Journal of Experimental Social Psychology*, 76 (2018) pp. 320–329.

Datu, J.A.D., G.S.P. Wong and C. Rubie-Davies, 'Can Kindness Promote Media Literacy Skills, Self-esteem, and Social Self-efficacy Among Selected Female Secondary School Students? An Intervention Study', *Computers & Education*, 161 (2021).

Davis, R., *Piers Plowman and the Books of Nature* (Oxford: Oxford University Press, 2016).

De Crescenzo, Luciano, *Il caffè sospeso: saggezza quotidiana in piccoli sorsi* (translated 'Suspended coffee: daily wisdom in small sips') (Milan: Mondadori, 2008).

de Souza, M., K. McLean, 'Bullying and Violence: Changing an Act of Disconnectedness into an Act of Kindness', *Pastoral Care in Education*, 30(2) (2012) pp. 165–180.

Dickerson, Revd Chris, 'An Epidemic of Kindness', *Carolina College of Biblical Studies* (2016) www.ccbs.edu/an-epidemic-of-kindness-2/ (accessed 30 December 2021).

Duncan, Deborah, Cathy Le Feuvre, *Lifelines* (Milton Keynes: Authentic, 2014).

Fowler, J.H., N.A. Christakis, 'Dynamic Spread of Happiness in a Large Social Network: Longitudinal Analysis Over 20 years in the Framingham Heart Study', *British Medical Journal* (2008) p. 337.

Fraser, I.D., 'Kindness: An Innate Ability of Potential Trainees?', *Journal of the Royal Society of Medicine*, 110(1) (2017) p. 4.

Fu, X., L.M. Padilla-Walker, M.N. Brown, 'Longitudinal Relations Between Adolescents' Self-esteem and Prosocial Behavior Toward Strangers, Friends and Family', *Journal of Adolescence*, 57 (2017) pp. 90–98.

Gilbert, P., Choden, *Mindful Compassion* (London: Robinson, 2013).

Haidt, Jonathan, 'Elevation and the Positive Psychology of Morality', in C.L.M. Keyes and J. Haidt, eds, *Flourishing: Positive Psychology and the Life Well-lived* (Washington DC: American Psychological Association, 2001) pp. 275–289.

Hamilton, David, 'Born to be kind', *David R Hamilton PhD* (2017) https://drdavidhamilton.com/born-to-be-kind/ (accessed 19 January 2022).

Hamilton, D.R., *The Five Side Effects of Kindness: This Book Will Make You Feel Better, Be Happier & Live Longer* (Carlsbad, CA: Hay House UK, 2017) p. 20.

Hamlin, J.K., K. Wynn, P. Bloom, 'Social Evaluation by Preverbal Infants', *Nature*, 450(7169) (2007) pp. 557–559.

Hardy Hammond, Lily, *In the Garden of Delight* (New York: Thomas Y. Crowell Co., 1916) p. 209. Archived from the original on 7 October 2012, www.archive.org/details/InTheGardenOfDelight/page/n221/mode/2up (accessed 15 January 2022).

Hasson, G., *Kindness* (Mankato, MN: Capstone, 2018) p. 19.

Henry, Matthew, 'Commentary on Acts 28', *Blue Letter Bible* (2022) www.blueletterbible.org/Comm/mhc/Act/Act_028.cfm (accessed 30 December 2021).

Hyde, C.R., *Pay it Forward* (New York, NY: Pocket Books, 2000).

Ingall, Alice, 'The Kindness Test: Sussex partners with BBC Radio 4 to explore the nation's attitudes to kindness', *University of Sussex* (2021) www.sussex.ac.uk/broadcast/read/55933 (accessed 31 December 2021).

IsHak, W.W., M. Davis, J. Jeffrey, K. Balayan, R.N. Pechnick, K. Bagot, M.H. Rapaport, 'The Role of Dopaminergic Agents in Improving Quality of Life in Major Depressive Disorder', *Current Psychiatry Reports*, 11(6) (2009) pp. 503–508.

Kaplan Thaler, Linda, Robin Koval, *The Power of Nice* (New York, NY: Crown Business, 2006).

Kindness UK™, Kindness Day UK™, https://kindnessuk.com/world_kindness_day_kindness_day_uk.php (accessed 30 December 2021).

LeRoy, Bridget, 'Is Kindness Contagious?', *World Tribune* (2016) www.worldtribune.org/2016/02/is-kindness-contagious/ (accessed 30 December 2021).

Llangollen International Musical Eisteddfod, 'Plymouth "Kindness Capital" of the UK' (2017) www.international-eisteddfod.co.uk/plymouth-kindness-capital-of-the-uk/ (accessed 30 December 2021).

Masterson, M.L., K.C. Kersey, 'Connecting Children to Kindness: Encouraging a Culture of Empathy', *Childhood Education*, 89(4) (2013) pp. 211–216.

Mautz, Scott, 'A Harvard Psychologist Says Kids Who Grow Up Kind Have Parents Who Do These 5 Things', *Inc.* (2022) www.inc.com/scott-mautz/want-to-raise-kind-children-a-harvard-psychologist-says-do-these-5-things.html (accessed 30 December 2021).

McLeod, Saul, 'Maslow's Hierachy of Needs', *Simply Psychology* (2020) www.simplypsychology.org/maslow.html (accessed 30 December 2021).

Nesterak, E., 'The End of Nature Versus Nurture', *Science* (2015) https://behavioralscientist.org/the-end-of-nature-versus-nurture/ (accessed 1 December 2021).

Newsworks, 'Daily Mirror celebrates hope with "1000 acts of kindness" campaign' (2021) www.newsworks.org.uk/news-and-opinion/daily-mirror-celebrates-hope-with-1000-acts-of-kindness-campaign/ (accessed 19 January 2022).

Nietzche, F., *Human, All Too Human* (trans. H. Zimmern; Edinburgh: T.N. Foulis, 1910) https://digitalassets.lib.berkeley.edu/main/b20790001_v_1_B000773557.pdf (accessed 19 January 2021).

NSW Agency for Clinical Innovation, 'Pandemic Kindness Movement' (2020) www.aci.health.nsw.gov.au/covid-19/kindness (accessed 30 December 2021).

Palgi, S., E. Klein, S.G. Shamay-Tsoory, 'Intranasal Administration of Oxytocin Increases Compassion Toward Women', *Social Cognitive and Affective Neuroscience*, 10(3) (2015) pp. 311–317.

Peteet, J.R., 'Struggles with God: Transference and Religious Countertransference in the Treatment of a Trauma Survivor', *Journal of the American Academy of Psychoanalysis and Dynamic Psychiatry*, 37 (2009) pp. 165–174.

Phillips, A., B. Taylor, *On Kindness* (London: Hamish Books, 2009).

Podsakoff, N.P., S.W. Whiting, P.M. Podsakoff, B.D. Blume, 'Individual- and organizational-level consequences of organizational citizenship behaviors: A meta-analysis', *Journal of Applied Psychology*, 94(1) (2009) pp. 122–141. https://doi.org/10.1037/a0013079 (accessed 16 January 2022).

Prosocial World (2021) www.prosocial.world (accessed 13 January 2022).

Ross, C.A., N. Halpern, *Trauma Model Therapy: A Treatment Approach for Trauma Dissociation and Complex Comorbidity* (Richardson, TX: Manitou Communications, 2009).

Roth-Hanania, R., M. Davidov, C. Zahn-Waxler, 'Empathy Development From 8 to 16 Months: Early Signs of Concern for Others', *Infant Behavior and Development*, 34(3) (2011) pp. 447–458.

Rowland, L., 'Kindness: Society's Golden Chain', *The Psychologist*, 31 (2018) pp. 30–35.

Sanders, Corinne, '17 Stories of Kindness During the Coronavirus Pandemic', *InspireMore* (2020) www.inspiremore.com/covid-19-stories-of-humanity/ (accessed 18 January 2022).

Sanders, Michael, Francesca Tamma, 'The science behind why people give money to charity', *The Guardian* (2015) www.theguardian.com/voluntary-sector-network/2015/mar/23/the-science-behind-why-people-give-money-to-charity (accessed 30 December 2021).

Sanfey, A.G., 'Social Decision-making: Insights From Game Theory and Neuroscience', *Science*, 318 (2007) pp. 598–602.

Sergio, Michele, 'Caffè sospeso, from the ancient Neapolitan habit to national phenomenon', *Gran Caffè Gambrinus* (2017) https://grancaffegambrinus.com/en/caffe-sospeso-from-the-ancient-neapolitan-habit-to-national-phenomenon/ (accessed 15 January 2022).

Sezer, O., K. Nault, N. Klein, 'Don't Underestimate the Power of Kindness at Work', *Harvard Business Review*, 2021, online, https://store.hbr.org/product/don-t-underestimate-the-power-of-kindness-at-work/H06C5G (accessed 30 December 2021).

Sheldon, C.M., *In His Steps: What Would Jesus Do?* (Chicago, IL: Advance Pub. Co., 1896).

Sheldon, C.M., *Jesus is Here* (New York, NY: Hodder & Stoughton/George H. Doran, 1914).

Sirota, M., 'The Difference Between Being Nice and Being Kind' (2016) www.huffingtonpost.ca/marcia-sirota/too-nice_b_946956.html (accessed 30 December 2021).

Snaith, Norman H., 'Loving Kindness', *Bible Research* (2012) www.bible-researcher.com/chesed.html (accessed 30 December 2021).

Sweeney, John M., 'A Passionate Journey', *Suspended Coffees* (2019) www.suspendedcoffees.com/a-passionate-journey/ (accessed 15 January 2022).

Tashjian, S.M., D.G. Weissman, A.E. Guyer, A. Galván, 'Neural Response to Prosocial Scenes Relates to Subsequent Giving Behavior in Adolescents: A Pilot Study', *Cognitive, Affective, & Behavioral Neuroscience*, 18(2) (2018) pp. 342–352.

Tse, W.S., A.J. Bond, 'Difference in Serotonergic and Noradrenergic Regulation of Human Social Behaviours', *Psychopharmacology*, 159 (2002) pp. 216–221.

Williams, Pamela A., 'The Kindness of Jesus', *When People are Kind* (2022) https://whenpeoplearekind.org/the-kindness-of-jesus/ (accessed 30 December 2021).

Notes

Foreword

1 Alice Ingall, 'The Kindness Test: Sussex partners with BBC Radio 4 to explore the nation's attitudes to kindness', *University of Sussex* (2021) www.sussex.ac.uk/broadcast/read/55933 (accessed 28 March 2022). The results are due to be published as this book goes to press.

2 For episodes see https://www.bbc.co.uk/programmes/m00154cp/episodes/player (accessed 29 March 2022).

3 Alice Ingall, 'Two thirds of people who took part in The Kindness Test think the pandemic has made people kinder', *University of Sussex* (2022) https://www.sussex.ac.uk/broadcast/read/57570 (accessed 30 March 2022).

4 Ibid.

5 Random Acts of Kindness Foundation, 'Kindness Quotes' (2022) https://www.randomactsofkindness.org/kindness-quotes/127-no-act-of-kindness-no (accessed 1 April 2022).

Chapter One

1 Robert Stevenson, *Virginibus Puerisque and Other Papers* (2012) The Project Gutenberg, https://www.gutenberg.org/files/386/386-h/386-h.htm (accessed 19 January 2022).

2 Definition taken from *Cambridge Academic Content Dictionary* © Cambridge University Press (2017) https://dictionary.cambridge.org/dictionary/english/kindness (accessed 1st October 2021). Reproduced with permission of The Licensor through PLSclear.

3 A. Cole-King, P. Gilbert, 'Compassionate Care: The Theory and the Reality', *Journal of Holistic Health Care* 8(3), (2011), pp. 29–37. http://www.connectingwithpeople.org/sites/default/files/Compassionate%20care%20ACK%20and%20PG.pdf (accessed 1 October 2021).

4 Lorette M. Enochs, *Seeds of Recovery: A Journal of 101 Mental Health Reflections* (Bloomington, IN: AuthorHouse, 2016) p. 76.

5 Aristotle (trans. Lee Honeycutt), 'Kindness', *Rhetoric*, Book II, chapter 7. Archived from the original on 13 December 2004, https://web.archive.org/web/20041213221951/http://www.public.iastate.edu/~honeyl/Rhetoric/rhet2-7.html (accessed 30 December 2021).

6 Y. Membray, 'The 10 Worse Britons in History', www.historyextra.com/period/medieval/the-10-worst-britons-in-history/ (accessed 30 December 2021).

7 For more information, see R. Davis, *Piers Plowman and the Books of Nature* (Oxford: Oxford University Press, 2016).

8 F. Nietzche, *Human, All Too Human* (trans. H. Zimmern; Edinburgh: T.N. Foulis, 1910), https://digitalassets.lib.berkeley.edu/main/b20790001_v_1_B000773557.pdf (accessed 19 January 2021).

9 Kindness UK™, Kindness Day UK™, https://kindnessuk.com/world_kindness_day_kindness_day_uk.php (accessed 30 December 2021).

10 Newsworks, 'Daily Mirror celebrates hope with "1000 acts of kindness" campaign' (2021) www.newsworks.org.uk/news-and-opinion/daily-mirror-celebrates-hope-with-1000-acts-of-kindness-campaign/ (accessed 19 January 2022).

11 For more information see www.simple.co.uk/stories-of-kindness/five-reasons-why-people-are-kind.html (accessed 30 December 2021).

12 C.R. Hyde, *Pay it Forward* (New York, NY: Pocket Books, 2000).

[13] Lily Hardy Hammond, *In the Garden of Delight* (New York: Thomas Y. Crowell Co., 1916), p. 209. Archived from the original on 7 October 2012, www.archive.org/details/InTheGardenOfDelight/page/n221/mode/2up (accessed 15 January 2022).

[14] For more details see https://payitforwardfoundation.org/ (accessed 30 December 2021).

[15] M. Sirota, 'The Difference Between Being Nice and Being Kind' (2016) www.huffingtonpost.ca/marcia-sirota/too-nice_b_946956.html (accessed 30 December 2021).

[16] Robert Stevenson, *Virginibus Puerisque and Other Papers* (2012) The Project Gutenberg, https://www.gutenberg.org/files/386/386-h/386-h.htm (accessed 19 January 2022).

[17] National Governors Association, 'Nebraska: Gov. Joseph Robert (Bob) Kerrey' (2022) www.nga.org/governor/joseph-robert-bob-kerrey/ (accessed 19 January 2022).

Chapter Two

[1] See 2 Corinthians 6:1–13; Galatians 5:22–23.

Chapter Three

[1] Pamela A. Williams, 'The Kindness of Jesus', *When People are Kind* (2022) https://whenpeoplearekind.org/the-kindness-of-jesus/ (accessed 30 December 2021).

[2] Professor Barry H. Corey, *Love Kindness: Discover the Power of a Forgotten Christian Virtue* (Wheaton, IL: Tyndale House, Publishers, Inc., 2016).

[3] Ibid., Introduction, p. 5.

[4] *Shayast-na-Shayast 13.29*, www.sacred-texts.com/zor/sbe05/sbe0507.htm#fr_49 via www.sacred-texts.com/zor/sbe05/index.htm (accessed 11 January 2022).

5 *Gleanings From the Writings of Bahá'u'lláh LXVI*, US Bahá'í Publishing Trust (1990) p. 126, www.reference.bahai.org/en/t/b/GWB/gwb-66.html (accessed 20 January 2022).
6 *Udana-Varga, 5:18*, attributed to the Buddha and his disciples, www.tibetanbuddhistencyclopedia.com/ (accessed 11 January 2022).
7 Confucius, *Analects 15.23*, www.confucius-1.com/analects/index.html (accessed 11 January 2022).
8 Vyasa, *Mahabharata: 5:1517*, www.worldhistory.org/Mahabharata/ and www.holybooks.com/mahabharata-all-volumes-in-12-pdf-files/ (accessed 12 January 2022).
9 Number 13 of Imam Al-Nawawi's *Forty Hadiths*, www.alim.org/hadith/nawawi/13/ (accessed 12 January 2022).
10 Maria MacLachlan, 'The Golden Rule', *Think Humanism* (2007) www.thinkhumanism.com/the-golden-rule (accessed 25 January 2022).
11 *Hillel, Talmud, Shabbat 31a*, www.come-and-hear.com/shabbath/shabbath_31.html (accessed 12 January 2022).
12 C.M. Sheldon, *In His Steps: What Would Jesus Do*? (Chicago, IL: Advance Pub. Co., 1896).
13 C.M. Sheldon, *Jesus is Here* (New York, NY: Hodder & Stoughton/George H. Doran, 1914).
14 Professor Barry H. Corey, *Love Kindness: Discover the Power of a Forgotten Christian Virtue* (Wheaton, IL: Tyndale House Publishers, 2016). Introduction, p. 6.

Chapter Four

1 C.N. Bovee, *Thoughts, Feelings and Fancies* (New York: Wiley and Halsted, 1857) p. 109.
2 J. Ballatt, P. Campling, 'Intelligent Kindness: Reforming the Culture of Healthcare' (London: RCPsych Publications, 2011).
3 P. Gilbert, Choden, *Mindful Compassion* (London: Robinson, 2013).

4 C.S. Carter. 'Oxytocin Pathways and the Evolution of Human Behaviour', *Annual Review of Psychology*, 65 (2014) pp. 17–39.

5 S. Palgi, E. Klein, S.G. Shamay-Tsoory, 'Intranasal Administration of Oxytocin Increases Compassion Toward Women', *Social Cognitive and Affective Neuroscience*, 10(3) (2015) pp. 311–317.

6 W.W. IsHak, M. Davis, J. Jeffrey, K. Balayan, R.N. Pechnick, K. Bagot and M.H. Rapaport, 'The Role of Dopaminergic Agents in Improving Quality of Life in Major Depressive Disorder', *Current Psychiatry Reports*, 11(6) (2009) pp. 503–508.

7 A.G. Sanfey, 'Social Decision-making: Insights From Game Theory and Neuroscience', *Science*, 318 (2007) pp. 598–602.

8 W.S. Tse, A.J. Bond, 'Difference in Serotonergic and Noradrenergic Regulation of Human Social Behaviours', *Psychopharmacology*, 159 (2002) pp. 216–221.

9 E. Cassell, *Oxford Handbook of Positive Psychology* (New York, NY: Oxford University Press, 2009, second edn) pp. 393–403.

10 L.B. Aknin, E.W. Dunn, J. Proulx, I. Lok, M.I. Norton, 'Does Spending Money on Others Promote Happiness?: A Registered Replication Report', *Journal of Personality and Social Psychology*, 119(2) (2020) e15–e26.

11 Michael Sanders and Francesca Tamma, 'The science behind why people give money to charity', *The Guardian* (2015) www.theguardian.com/voluntary-sector-network/2015/mar/23/the-science-behind-why-people-give-money-to-charity (accessed 30 December 2021).

12 G. Hasson, *Kindness* (Mankato, MN: Capstone, 2018) p. 19.

13 R. Francis, 'Report of the Mid Staffordshire Trust Public Inquiry: Executive Summary' (2013) https://assets.publishing.service.gov.uk/government/uploads/system/uploads/attachment_data/file/279124/0947.pdf (accessed 30 December 2021).

14 Ibid.

15 See P. Campling. 'Reforming the Culture of Healthcare: The Case for Intelligent Kindness', *BJPsych Bulletin*, 39(1) (2015) pp. 1–5.

16 Ibid.

Chapter Five

1 John 15:12–13; 1 Pet. 2:9; Deut. 7:6; Ps. 17:8; Luke 12:7; Jer. 1:5.

2 X. Fu, L.M. Padilla-Walker, M.N. Brown, 'Longitudinal Relations Between Adolescents' Self-esteem and Prosocial Behavior Toward Strangers, Friends and Family', *Journal of Adolescence*, 57 (2017) pp. 90–98.

3 J.A.D. Datu, G.S.P. Wong and C. Rubie-Davies, 'Can Kindness Promote Media Literacy Skills, Self-esteem, and Social Self-efficacy Among Selected Female Secondary School Students? An Intervention Study', *Computers & Education*, 161 (2021).

4 S.M. Tashjian, D.G. Weissman, A.E. Guyer, A. Galván, 'Neural Response to Prosocial Scenes Relates to Subsequent Giving Behavior in Adolescents: A Pilot Study', *Cognitive, Affective, & Behavioral Neuroscience* 18(2) (2018) pp. 342–352.

5 The Prayer Foundation, 'Serenity Prayer' (2010) www.prayerfoundation.org/dailyoffice/serenity_prayer_full_version.htm (accessed 11 January 2022).

6 Bridget LeRoy, 'Is Kindness Contagious?', *World Tribune* (2016) www.worldtribune.org/2016/02/is-kindness-contagious (accessed 30 December 2021).

7 J.H. Fowler, N.A. Christakis, 'Dynamic Spread of Happiness in a Large Social Network: Longitudinal Analysis Over 20 years in the Framingham Heart Study', *British Medical Journal* (2008) p. 337.

Chapter Six

1 Amelia Earhart, 'Quotes' (2021) https://ameliaearhart.com/index.php/quotes/ (accessed 10 February 2022).

2 Random Acts of Kindness Foundation, 'Kindness Quotes' (2022) https://www.randomactsofkindness.org/kindness-quotes/88-kindness-is-the-golden-chain (accessed 11 February 2022). See Johann Wolfgang von Goethe's works at Projekt Gutenberg: https://www.projekt-gutenberg.org/autoren/namen/goethe.html (accessed 11 February 2022).

3 J. Chancellor, S. Margolis, K. Jacobs Bao, S. Lyubomirsky, 'Everyday prosociality in the workplace: The reinforcing benefits of giving, getting, and glimpsing', *Emotion* (Washington, DC), 18(4) (2018). Retrieved from https://escholarship.org/uc/item/9t0213nd (accessed 13 January 2022).

4 Kendra Cherry, 'The Basics of Prosocial Behavior', *Verywell Mind* (2020) www.verywellmind.com/what-is-prosocial-behavior-2795479 (accessed 30 December 2021).

5 Prosocial World (2021) www.prosocial.world (accessed 13 January 2022).

6 Ibid.

7 Ibid.

8 J. Chancellor, S. Margolis, K. Jacobs Bao and S. Lyubomirsky, 'Everyday prosociality in the workplace: The reinforcing benefits of giving, getting, and glimpsing' (2018) pp. 507–517. http://dx.doi.org/10.1037/emo0000321 Retrieved from https://escholarship.org/uc/item/9t0213nd (accessed 13 January 2022).

9 Ibid.

10 © Rutger Bregman 2020, Translation © Elizabeth Manton and Erica Moore, 'Humankind: A Hopeful History', Bloomsbury Publishing Plc.

11 Bregman, *Humankind*, Chapter 1.

12 Bregman, *Humankind*, Epilogue.

13 Bregman, *Humankind*, Epilogue.

14 Jonathan Haidt, 'Elevation and the Positive Psychology of Morality', in C.L.M. Keyes and J. Haidt, eds, *Flourishing: Positive Psychology and the Life Well-lived* (Washington DC: American Psychological Association, 2001) pp. 275–289.

15 Bregman, *Humankind*, Epilogue.

16 www.prosocial.world (accessed 13 January 2022).

Chapter Seven

1 Random Acts of Kindness Foundation, 'Kindness Quotes' (2022) https://www.randomactsofkindness.org/kindness-quotes/127-no-act-of-kindness-no (accessed 10 February 2022).

2 NSW Agency for Clinical Innovation, 'Pandemic Kindness Movement' (2020) www.aci.health.nsw.gov.au/covid-19/kindness (accessed 30 December 2021).

3 Saul McLeod, 'Maslow's Hierachy of Needs', *Simply Psychology* (2020) www.simplypsychology.org/maslow.html (accessed 30 December 2021).

4 NSW Agency for Clinical Innovation, 'Pandemic Kindness Movement: Love and belonging' (2020) www.aci.health.nsw.gov.au/covid-19/kindness/love (accessed 30 December 2021).

5 Local BBC Radio, 'Make a Difference' *BBC*, (2022) https://www.bbc.co.uk/programmes/articles/5SqHJMTKZx5sYhlltXJvB1Q/give-a-laptop (accessed 11 February 2022).

6 Marie-Claire Chappet, 'How to *actually* be kind during the Coronavirus pandemic: Let's ensure this sense of community long outlasts the pandemic', *Glamour UK*, www.glamourmagazine.co.uk/article/kindness-in-the-time-of-coronavirus (accessed 30 December 2021).

7 Bailiwick Express, 'Jersey's Bailiff recognises covid community heroes' (2020) www.bailiwickexpress.com/jsy/news/covid-helpers-recognised-bailiff (accessed 30 December 2021).

8 Good News Network, 'Teen Has Performed a Random Act of Kindness Every Day Since the Start of the Pandemic' (2021) www.goodnewsnetwork.org/teen-has-performed-a-random-act-of-kindness-every-day-since-the-start-of-the-pandemic/ (accessed 18 January 2022).

9 Shermaine Ang, '"Kindness tree", food drive for the needy among student-led initiatives that bag awards', *The Straits Times* (2022) www.straitstimes.com/singapore/community/kindness-tree-food-drive-for-the-needy-among-student-led-initiatives-that-bag-awards (accessed 18 January 2022).

10 Corinne Sanders, '17 Stories of Kindness During the Coronavirus Pandemic', *InspireMore* (2020) www.inspiremore.com/covid-19-stories-of-humanity/ (accessed 18 January 2022).

Chapter Eight

1 BBC, 'Tintern Abbey by William Wordsworth' (2014) https://www.bbc.co.uk/poetryseason/poems/tintern_abbey.shtml (accessed 10 February 2022).

2 J.K. Hamlin, K. Wynn, P. Bloom, 'Social Evaluation by Preverbal Infants', *Nature*, 450(7169) (2007) pp. 557–559.

3 I.D. Fraser, 'Kindness: An Innate Ability of Potential Trainees?', *Journal of the Royal Society of Medicine*, 110(1) (2017) p. 4.

4 David Hamilton, 'Born to be kind', *David R Hamilton PhD* (2017) https://drdavidhamilton.com/born-to-be-kind/ (accessed 19 January 2022).

5 P. Bloom, 'Morality Special: Infant Origins of Human Kindness', *New Scientist*, 208(2782) (2010) pp. 44–45.

6 P. Bloom, 'The Moral Life of Babies', *New York Times Magazine* (2019) https://www.nytimes.com/2010/05/09/magazine/09babies-t.html (accessed 1 December 2021).

7 E. Nesterak, 'The End of Nature Versus Nurture', *Science* (2015) https://behavioralscientist.org/the-end-of-nature-versus-nurture/ (accessed 1 December 2021).

8 J.R. Peteet, 'Struggles with God: Transference and Religious Countertransference in the Treatment of a Trauma Survivor', *Journal of the American Academy of Psychoanalysis and Dynamic Psychiatry*, 37 (2009) pp. 165–174.

9 C.A. Ross, N. Halpern, *Trauma Model Therapy: A Treatment Approach for Trauma Dissociation and Complex Comorbidity* (Richardson, TX: Manitou Communications, 2009).

10 Linda Kaplan Thaler, Robin Koval, *The Power of Nice* (New York, NY: Crown Business, 2006).

11 R. Roth-Hanania, M. Davidov, C. Zahn-Waxler, 'Empathy Development From 8 to 16 Months: Early Signs of Concern for Others', *Infant Behavior and Development*, 34(3) (2011) pp. 447–458.

12 M.L. Masterson, K.C. Kersey, 'Connecting Children to Kindness: Encouraging a Culture of Empathy', *Childhood Education*, 89(4) (2013) pp. 211–216.

13 L. Rowland, 'Kindness: Society's Golden Chain', *The Psychologist*, 31 (2018) pp. 30–35.

14 Ibid.

15 D. Canter, D. Youngs, M. Yaneva, 'Towards a Measure of Kindness: An Exploration of a Neglected Interpersonal Trait', *Personality and Individual Differences*, 106 (2017) pp. 15–20.

16 A. Phillips, B. Taylor, *On Kindness* (London: Hamish Books, 2009).

17 O.S. Curry, L.A. Rowland, C.J. Van Lissa, S. Zlotowitz, J. McAlaney, H. Whitehouse, 'Happy to Help? A Systematic Review and Meta-analysis of the Effects of Performing Acts of Kindness on the Well-being of the Actor', *Journal of Experimental Social Psychology*, 76 (2018) pp. 320–329.

18 D.R. Hamilton, *The Five Side Effects of Kindness: This Book Will Make You Feel Better, Be Happier & Live Longer* (Carlsbad, CA: Hay House UK, 2017) p. 20.

19 J. Peters, 'Bloomberg Plans a $50 Million Challenge to the N.R.A.', *The New York Times* (2014) www.nytimes.com/2014/04/16/us/bloomberg-plans-a-50-million-challenge-to-the-nra.html (accessed 31 December 2021).

20 M. Mead, Epigraph of Chapter VI: The Politics of Consciousness, in Donald Keys, *Earth at Omega: Passage to Planetization* (Boston, MA: Branden Press, 1982) p. 79.

21 Matt Liddy, 'Australia Talks can help you understand how you compare to other Australians – here's how', *ABC News* (2019) www.abc.net.au/news/2019-10-06/australia-talks-explained/11570332 (accessed 31 December 2021).

22 K. Baskerville, K. Johnson, E. Monk-Turner, Q. Slone, H. Standley, S. Stansbury . . . J. Young, 'Reactions to Random Acts of Kindness', *The Social Science Journal*, 37(2) (2000) pp. 293–298.

Chapter Nine

1 William Cabell Bruce, *Benjamin Franklin; Self-Revealed: A Biographical and Critical Study Based Mainly on His Own Writings*, Vol. 1 (New York; London: G.P. Putnam's Sons, The Knickerbocker Press, 1917) p. 151, www.gutenberg.org/files/36896/36896-h/36896-h.htm (accessed 10 February 2022).

2 Michele Sergio, 'Caffè sospeso, from the ancient Neapolitan habit to national phenomenon', *Gran Caffè Gambrinus* (2017) https://grancaffegambrinus.com/en/caffe-sospeso-from-the-ancient-neapolitan-habit-to-national-phenomenon/ (accessed 15 January 2022).

3 Classical Literature, 'Dyskolos' (www.ancient-literature.com/greece_menander_dyskolos.html (accessed 15 January 2022).

4 Michele Sergio, 'Caffè sospeso, from the ancient Neapolitan habit to national phenomenon', *Gran Caffè Gambrinus* (2017) https://grancaffegambrinus.com/en/caffe-sospeso-from-the-ancient-neapolitan-habit-to-national-phenomenon/ (accessed 15 January 2022).

5 Luciano De Crescenzo, *Il caffè sospeso: saggezza quotidiana in piccoli sorsi* (translated 'Suspended coffee: daily wisdom in small sips') (Milan: Mondadori, 2008).

6 United Nations, 'Human Rights Day 10 December' (2021) www.un.org/en/observances/human-rights-day (accessed 30 December 2021).

7 John M. Sweeney, 'A Passionate Journey', *Suspended Coffees* (2019) www.suspendedcoffees.com/a-passionate-journey/ (accessed 15 January 2022).

8 Suspended Coffees, *Facebook* (2022) https://www.facebook.com/SuspendedCoffeess (accessed 15 January 2022).

9 Encyclopedic Dictionary of Bible and Theology, 'Hammond, Lily Hardy (1859–1925)', www.biblia.work/dictionaries/hammondlily-hardy-1859-1925/ (accessed 15 January 2022).

10 Lily Hardy Hammond, *In the Garden of Delight*, p. 209. Archived from the original by 'Internet Archive' on 7 October 2012, www.archive.org/details/InTheGardenOfDelight/page/n221/mode/2up (accessed 15 January 2022).

11 Pay It Forward Foundation, www.payitforwardfoundation.org/thoughtful-giving/ (accessed 30 December 2021).

12 Warner Bros. Entertainment Inc., *Pay it Forward* (2000) www.warnerbros.com/movies/pay-it-forward (accessed 15 January 2022).

[13] Lily Hardy Hammond, *In the Garden of Delight*, p. 209. Archived from the original by 'Internet Archive' on 7 October 2012, www.archive.org/details/InTheGardenOfDelight/page/n221/mode/2up (accessed 15 January 2022).

[14] Revd Chris Dickerson, 'An Epidemic of Kindness', *Carolina College of Biblical Studies* (2016) www.ccbs.edu/an-epidemic-of-kindness-2/ (accessed 30 December 2021).

[15] Ibid.

[16] Ibid.

[17] Ibid.

[18] Ibid.

[19] Ibid.

[20] Ibid.

[21] Anti-bullying Alliance, 'Anti-Bullying Week 2021: One Kind Word' *National Children's Bureau* (2022) (www.anti-bullyingalliance.org.uk/anti-bullying-week/anti-bullying-week-2021-one-kind-word (accessed 30 December 2021).

[22] Ibid.

[23] O. Sezer, K. Nault, N. Klein, 'Don't Underestimate the Power of Kindness at Work', *Harvard Business Review* (2021) online, https://store.hbr.org/product/don-t-underestimate-the-power-of-kindness-at-work/H06C5G (accessed 30 December 2021).

[24] Ibid.

[25] Ibid.

[26] N.P. Podsakoff, S.W. Whiting, P.M. Podsakoff, B.D. Blume, 'Individual- and organizational-level consequences of organizational citizenship behaviors: A meta-analysis', *Journal of Applied Psychology*, 94(1) (2009) 122–141. https://doi.org/10.1037/a0013079 (accessed 16 January 2022).

[27] O. Sezer, K. Nault, N. Klein' 'Don't Underestimate the Power of Kindness at Work', *Harvard Business Review (*2021) online, https://store.hbr.org/product/don-t-underestimate-the-power-of-kindness-at-work/H06C5G (accessed 30 December 2021).

[28] Ibid.

[29] Ibid.

[30] Ibid.

Chapter Ten

1 Rowland, 'Kindness: Society's Golden Chain', pp. 30–35.

2 Matthew Henry, 'Commentary on Acts 28', *Blue Letter Bible* (2022) www.blueletterbible.org/Comm/mhc/Act/Act_028.cfm (accessed 30 December 2021).

3 Scott Mautz, 'A Harvard Psychologist Says Kids Who Grow Up Kind Have Parents Who Do These 5 Things', *Inc.* (2022) www.inc.com/scott-mautz/want-to-raise-kind-children-a-harvard-psychologist-says-do-these-5-things.html (accessed 30 December 2021).

4 Harvard Graduate School of Education, 'Richard Weissbourd' (2022) www.gse.harvard.edu/faculty/richard-weissbourd (accessed 19 January 2022).

5 M. de Souza, K. McLean, 'Bullying and Violence: Changing an Act of Disconnectedness into an Act of Kindness', *Pastoral Care in Education*, 30(2) (2012) pp. 165–180.

6 Deborah Duncan, Cathy Le Feuvre, *Lifelines* (Milton Keynes: Authentic, 2014).

7 Fables of Aesop, 'The Lion and the Mouse', *Tom Simondi* (2016) 'https://fablesofaesop.com/the-lion-and-the-mouse.html (accessed 11 January 2022).

8 Norman H. Snaith, 'Loving Kindness', *Bible Research* (2012) www.bible-researcher.com/chesed.html (accessed 30 December 2021).

9 Trent C. Butler, Editor, entry for 'Kindness', *Holman Bible Dictionary* (1991) www.studylight.org/dictionaries/eng/hbd/k/kindness.html (accessed 11 January 2022).

10 Llangollen International Musical Eisteddfod, 'Plymouth "Kindness Capital" of the UK' (2017) www.international-eisteddfod.co.uk/plymouth-kindness-capital-of-the-uk/ (accessed 30 December 2021).

11 Ibid. Original list edited for the purposes of this book.

12 Ibid.

13 Ibid.

[14] Alice Ingall, 'The Kindness Test: Sussex partners with BBC Radio 4 to explore the nation's attitudes to kindness', *University of Sussex* (2021) www.sussex.ac.uk/broadcast/read/55933 (accessed 31 December 2021).

[15] Ibid.

Life Lines

Two friends sharing laughter, challenges and cupcakes

Deborah Duncan and Cathy Le Feuvre

This is the story of Esther and Louise, two women who share the good times and the bad, the experiences that make their hearts soar, and those moments when they feel they inhabit a different planet to those around them.

With gentle humour, it unearths the ridiculous things that happen in life and church while celebrating the joys of Christian community. It's a powerful portrayal of friendship forged in the tough times as well as the good, which prods and pokes but, most importantly, pushes the characters closer to the God they love.

978-1-86024-930-3

Minor Prophets, Major Prayer

Getting real with God

Deborah Duncan

Many of us want to pray but are unsure how to go about it.

Buried deep in the Bible, the Minor Prophets contain pearls of wisdom that form the raw material of prayer. These prophets understood the power of prayer, so what made them turn to God and how did they ask him for help?

By looking at each minor prophet in turn, Debbie Duncan explores their background and looks at how their example can help us to pray effectively today. They may be 'minor' prophets, but they teach us major truths about prayer.

978-1-78893-121-2

Be – Godly Wisdom to Live By

365 devotions for women

Fiona Castle and friends

Jesus gave us the greatest love of all. We are called not just to keep it to ourselves, but to overflow with that love to others. But how can we really do that in the busyness of our lives?

In these daily devotions, women from many walks of life share insights on scripture and practical life lessons to gently encourage you to live for Jesus, and to be more like him in your thoughts, character, and actions.

Discover godly wisdom that will help you navigate the world as a Christian woman and live out God's unique purpose for your life.

978-1-78893-239-4

A-Z of Wellbeing

Finding your personal toolkit for peace and wholeness

Ruth Rice

A-Z of Wellbeing is an accessible introduction to help you attend to your own wellbeing and live out your own alphabet of peace. It presents twenty-six words of wellness to help you discover new practices, connect with God, and share wellbeing with others.

Each topic guides the reader to:

- Connect the word to a biblical theme
- Learn a new habit to practise
- Get active sharing the habit with others
- Take notice of a personal story
- Give back with questions and further resources

By sharing the words that were helpful in her own journey of recovery from breakdown, Ruth Rice gently encourages us to find our own toolkit of words and habits that will help us maintain our own wellbeing.

978-1-78893-237-0

We trust you enjoyed reading this book from Authentic. If you want to be informed of any new titles from this author and other releases you can sign up to the Authentic newsletter by scanning below:

Online:
authenticmedia.co.uk

Follow us: